YORKSHIRE LANDSCAPES

YORKSHIRE LANDSCAPES

PHOTOGRAPHY BY ROB TALBOT
TEXT BY ROBIN WHITEMAN

 PHOENIX ILLUSTRATED

First published in 1998 by
George Weidenfeld & Nicolson Ltd

This paperback edition first published in 1999 by
Phoenix Illustrated
Orion Publishing Group, Orion House
5, Upper St. Martin's Lane
London WC2H 9EA

British Library Cataloguing-in-Publication Data
A catalogue record for this book is available from the British Library
ISBN 0-75380-705-X

Designed by Harry Green

Printed and bound in Italy

Other books by Talbot & Whiteman

THE COTSWOLDS

THE ENGLISH LAKES

THE YORKSHIRE MOORS & DALES

THE HEART OF ENGLAND

THE WEST COUNTRY

WESSEX

THE GARDEN OF ENGLAND

EAST ANGLIA & THE FENS

THE PEAK DISTRICT

SHAKESPEARE'S AVON

CADFAEL COUNTRY

BROTHER CADFAEL'S HERB GARDEN

ENGLISH LANDSCAPES

LAKELAND LANDSCAPES

Photographs by Talbot

SHAKESPEARE COUNTRY

THE LAKELAND POETS

COTSWOLD VILLAGES

Text by Whiteman

THE CADFAEL COMPANION

Half-title: WAYWORTH MOOR. In Forty Years in a Moorland Parish, the Rev. Atkinson extolled the beauty of the moors: 'It is not only in winter time, or when the hills are snow-draped and the dales snow-clad, that the marvels of beautiful colouring are displayed for the delight of the watching eye. A hundred times, and again a hundred, I have seen in the early autumn evenings, when the sun was sinking behind the western banks, all the moorland heights towards the east and north, as they rose in their receding order, take on the most lovely and delicate hues . . .' Yet, having seen the 'moors-scape a thousand times before', he still managed to come across a scene that left him astonished and amazed at 'the glory it might wear when gorgeously apparelled in array of Nature's own garnishing'.

Title-page: INGLEBOROUGH, FROM WHITE SCARS. Described by Thomas Gray as 'that huge monster of nature', Ingleborough, at 2,373 feet above sea-level, is the second highest mountain in post-1974 Yorkshire. It is also one of the noted 'Three Peaks of Yorkshire'; the others being nearby Whernside (2,419 feet) and Pen-y-ghent (2,273 feet). Despite being called 'peaks', their summits are either flat or gently rounded. Although limestone dominates the area, the geological structure of Ingleborough is essentially a gigantic sandwich: at the bottom, a 600-feet-thick bed of limestone; at the top, a 100-feet-thick slab of millstone grit; and between, 1,000 feet of shales and sandstones. On its summit stand the remains of the highest Iron Age fort in Britain. While on its south-eastern flank is the famous Gaping Gill pothole.

ACKNOWLEDGEMENTS

Robin Whiteman and Rob Talbot would particularly like to acknowledge the generous co-operation of English Heritage (Historic Properties North) and the National Trust (Yorkshire Region) in allowing them to take photographs of their properties. They are also extremely grateful to the following: Castle Howard Estate Ltd. and the Hon. Simon Howard; the Earl of Harewood, Harewood House, near Leeds; Ampleforth Abbey Trust; and The Trustees of the Chatsworth Settlement, Yorkshire Estate, Bolton Abbey.

Many thanks go to those people, mostly from Whitby, who responded so helpfully to our request (published in the Whitby Gazette) for information on the 'Creteblock'; especially David and Stephen Boocock of Whitby, Michael Pemberton of Leeds (a ferrocement specialist), Malcolm Barker of Harrogate, John C. Middleton of Whitby, David Green of Loftus, Keith Richardson of Saltburn-by-Sea, and J. R. Short of Whitby. (It should be noted, however, that responsibility for the accuracy of information on this wreck, as published in this book, rests solely with the author.) Thanks also to Meg Sloan, Keighley Reference Library for information on the Earl Crag monuments. Appreciation goes also to all those other individuals and organizations too numerous to mention by name who, nevertheless, made such a valuable contribution. Special thanks for making this book possible go to Michael Dover, at Weidenfeld & Nicolson, and Ted Smart, at the Book People.

CONTENTS

6   INTRODUCTION

24   MAP OF YORKSHIRE

26   *A TOUR THROUGH THE RIDINGS*

154   *THE NATIONAL PARKS*

155   SELECTED PROPERTIES & REGIONAL OFFICES

156   PHOTOGRAPHIC INFORMATION

158   BIBLIOGRAPHY

159   INDEX

Introduction

'If you've seen Yorkshire,' it has been said (by those who just so happen to live there), 'you've seen England.' The assertion may be something of an exaggeration, but within it lies an element of truth. Where else, within such a similarly small and compact region, can you find a landscape of such astonishing richness, beauty and diversity, or a heritage with such a wealth of history, life and traditions?

From the busy industrial towns and cities of the south-west to the wild coastal moorland of the north-east; from the rich fertile plains of the south-east to the barren limestone hills of the north-west; glorious ruins, such as the abbeys of Fountains and Rievaulx; stately mansions, like Castle Howard and Harewood House; ancient castles; enchanting villages; historic buildings; secluded dales; deep, plunging ravines; and flower-strewn meadows – Yorkshire has them all, and more, in abundance.

In short, Yorkshire contains some of the finest examples of both natural and man-made scenery in the country, encompassing two National Parks (the North York Moors and the Yorkshire Dales) as well as its much-celebrated 'capital' – the medieval city of York. Yorkshire also has a history steeped in legend, folklore and romance, and one renowned around the world for its literary and artistic associations. For the purpose of this book, Yorkshire – the largest county in England – is defined by its pre-1974 boundary: before parts of the county were incorporated into Cumbria, Lancashire and Durham; and before its three historic 'ridings' (from the Anglo-Saxon *thriding*, meaning a third part of something) fell victim to government reorganization.

To promote tourism in more recent times, the county has been subdivided into areas connected with real, historical people or fictional characters from popular television series: 'Summer Wine Country', 'Captain Cook Country', 'Brontë Country', 'Herriot Country', 'Heartbeat Country' and the like. Yorkshire is indeed the county of 'Countries'. Little wonder that Michael Drayton called it 'the most renowned of shires'.

In 1697, Celia Fiennes travelled through Yorkshire recording her impressions in a hand-written journal, an incomplete and inaccurate version of which was first published in 1888 under the title *Through England on a Side Saddle in the Time of William and Mary*. During her travels – made at a leisurely pace between about 1685 and 1703 – she explored every county in England, revisiting Yorkshire in 1698 on her 'Great Journey to Newcastle and to Cornwall'. The resulting document, written in a simple, lively and direct style, provides an important first-hand account of England at the close of the seventeenth century: when 'taking the waters' at spas was becoming fashionable; when London's main streets were first lit with oil lamps; when highwaymen were on the ascendant; and when roads (having deteriorated through neglect after the Dissolution of the Monasteries) were little more than earthen tracks, and impassable quagmires after heavy rain. In areas of the country where clay predominates, such as parts of Sussex and the Midlands, it was even said that the people and animals had grown long-legged through pulling their feet out of the stiff, sticky ground.

Although England's first turnpike was built on the Old North Road in 1663 – with a toll gate at Wadesmill, near Ware, in Hertfordshire – toll roads did not come into general operation until the following century. Due to the poor state of the roads, travelling by stagecoach during the time of William and Mary was both slow and hazardous. For long journeys most people, including Celia Fiennes, used horses rather than carts. Nevertheless, despite the increase of wheeled traffic, which rapidly worsened the condition of the highways, most goods were carried by long trains of pack animals.

In *The History of England* (1848) Lord Macaulay wrote: 'On byroads, and generally throughout the country north of York, and west of Exeter, goods were carried by long trains of packhorses. These strong and patient beasts, the breed of which is now extinct, were attended by a class of men who seemed to have borne much resemblance to the Spanish muleteers. A traveller of humble condition often found it convenient to perform a journey mounted on a packsaddle between two baskets, under the care of these hardy guides. The expense of this mode of conveyance was small. But the caravan moved at a foot's pace; and in winter the cold was unsupportable.'

The fastest method of travel in Celia Fiennes' time was the 'flying coach' which, according to Macaulay, ran: 'thrice a week from London to the chief towns . . . The ordinary day's journey . . . was about fifty miles in the summer; but in winter, when the ways were bad and the nights long, little more than thirty.'

There was also the added danger of being robbed by highwaymen. 'Whatever might be the way in which a journey was performed, the travellers, unless they were numerous and well-armed, ran considerable risk of being stopped and plundered. The mounted highwayman, a marauder known to our generation only from books, was to be found on every main road . . . Thus it was related of William Nevison, the great robber of Yorkshire, that he levied a quarterly tribute on all the northern drovers, and, in return, not only spared them himself, but protected them against all other thieves; that he demanded purses in the most courteous manner; that he gave largely to the poor what he had taken from the rich; that his life was once spared by the royal clemency, but that he again tempted his fate, and at length died, in 1685, on the gallows of York.'

A strict Nonconformist, Celia Fiennes was born on 7 June 1662, almost certainly at Newton Toney near Salisbury – the home of her father Colonel Nathaniel Fiennes, son of William, 1st Viscount Saye and Sele, and a staunch Parliamentarian who fought at Edge Hill and sat in Cromwell's equivalent of the House of Lords. On most of her journeys – invariably made alone (apart from one or two servants), riding side-saddle and carrying her own bed linen (not trusting the cleanliness of that supplied by the innkeepers) – she revealed an almost obsessional preoccupation with the state of her health. Indeed, her journeys, as she admitted herself, 'were begun to regain my health by variety and change of air and exercise'.

ROMAN ROAD, BLACKSTONE EDGE

Travelling from Rochdale to Halifax, in the 'middle of August', Daniel Defoe encountered snow on Blackstone Edge – where there are the well-preserved remains of a paved road thought to be Roman (some, however, claim it is medieval). 'It is not easy to express the consternation we were in when we came up near the top of the mountain; the wind blew exceeding hard, and blew the snow directly in our faces, and that so thick, that it was impossible to keep our eyes open to see our way. The ground was also covered with snow, that we could see no track . . . except when we were showed it by a frightful precipice on one hand, and uneven ground on the other; even our horses discovered their uneasiness at it; and and a poor spaniel dog . . . turned tail to it and cried.'

At every opportunity she would visit the 'spaws', maintaining that she had 'drank many years with great advantage'. Nor could she resist bathing in the 'exceeding cold water' of St Mungo's Well at Copgrove, five miles south-east of Ripon. 'I dipped my head quite over every time I went in and found it eased a great pain I used to have in my head, and I was not apt to catch cold so much as before . . . I went in seven several seasons and seven times every season and would have gone in oftener could we have stayed longer.'

In the vicinity of Harrogate she found four different types of spring water, including one, 'the sulphur or stinking spa', from which she 'drank a quart in a morning for two days and hold them to be a good sort of purge, if you can hold your breath so as to drink them down'.

Her tour in 1697 took her, among other places, to: Doncaster ('a pretty large town of stone buildings, the streets are good'); Pontefract ('built on a hill all of stone, it's a very neat building and the streets well pitched [sloped] and broad'); Tadcaster ('a very good little town for travellers, mostly inns and little tradesmen's houses'); Boroughbridge ('a famous place for salmon'); Burton Agnes ('the seat of Sir Griffith Boynton, grandson to Sir Francis which married my father's sister'); Scarborough ('a very pretty seaport town, built on the side of a high hill'); and York ('for one of the Metropolis and the See of the Archbishop it makes but a mean appearance, the streets are narrow and not of any length, save one which you enter of from the bridge, that is over the Ouse').

In general, however, unlike Fiennes, most of the inhabitants of England seldom ventured beyond a ten-mile radius of their home and, therefore, had no real appreciation of travelling distance. To confuse matters more, the further north Fiennes went, the longer the measurement of the mile became. Although the statute mile of 1,760 yards was defined in 1593, local variations on the length of the mile still persisted. The old Scottish mile was often 1,976 yards, and the old Irish mile 2,240 yards.

After making the fifteen-statute-mile journey from York to Aberford, by way of Tadcaster, 'all on a heavy bottom', she added: 'These miles are long and I observe the ordinary people both in these parts of Yorkshire and in the northern parts can scarce tell you how far it is to the next place unless it be in the great towns and there

in their public houses; and they tell you its good gait, instead of saying it is good way, and they call their gates yates, and do not esteem it uphill unless so steep as a house or precipice; they say its good level gait all along, when it may be there are several great hills to pass, but this account did increase on us the nearer we came to Derbyshire, but in general they live much at home and scarce ever go two or ten mile from thence, especially the women, so may be termed good housekeepers.'

Like Daniel Defoe after her – the account of his travels was published in *A Tour Thro' the Whole of Great Britain* (1724–26) – Fiennes crossed the Yorkshire moorland of Blackstone Edge, where there are the well-preserved remains of an ancient causeway, thought to be Roman in origin: 'Then I came to Blackstone Edge, noted all over England for a dismal high precipice and steep in the ascent and descent at either end . . . As I ascended the morning was pretty fair, but a sort of mist met me and small rain just as I attained the top . . . But when I attained the top – where is a great heap raised up which parts Yorkshire, and there I entered Lancashire – the mist began to lessen.'

Celia Fiennes died on 10 April 1741 at the age of seventy-eight. In her will she apologized for the diminution of the size and value of her estate, but made no mention of her journal. Nevertheless, as the manuscript was designed for 'my near relatives', not for publication, she could not resist offering them a little advise: 'If all persons, both ladies, much more gentlemen, would spend some of their time in journeys to visit their native land, and be curious to inform themselves and make observations of the pleasant prospects, good buildings, different produces and manufactures of each place . . . would be a sovereign remedy to cure or preserve from these epidemic diseases of vapours, should I add laziness? It would also form such an idea of England, add much glory and esteem in our minds and cure the evil itch of overvaluing foreign parts.'

In 1797, Joseph Mallord William Turner travelled through Yorkshire recording his impressions in a leather-bound sketchbook (now in the Turner Bequest at the Tate Gallery, London). During this north-of-England tour, made over a period of about eight weeks, he also visited Derbyshire, Durham, Northumberland, Berwick-upon-Tweed, the Scottish Borders, the Lake District, Lancashire and Lincolnshire. Not only was it the first of many such explorations to the north (he had already toured areas in the south), it was also one of the most important tours in his career as a landscape painter. In *Modern Painters*, in which he passionately championed Turner, John Ruskin described the point where he believed the artist discovered himself and the inspiration for his future works.

'And at last fortune wills that the lad's true life shall begin; and one summer's evening, after various wonderful stagecoach experiences on the north road, which gave him a love of stagecoaches ever after, he finds himself sitting alone among the Yorkshire hills. For the first time, the silence of Nature round him, her freedom sealed to him, her glory opened to him. Peace at last; no roll of cartwheel, nor mutter of sullen voices in the back shop; but curlew-cry in space of heaven, and welling of bell-toned streamlet by its shadowy rock. Freedom at last.'

It is generally acknowledged that Turner's experience of dawn breaking at Norham Castle, on the English bank of the River Tweed in Northumberland, brought him a new awareness of atmosphere and light, from which he was to draw inspiration throughout his life. Yet, in Ruskin's opinion, the place which influenced Turner most was Yorkshire:

'I do not know in what district of England Turner first or longest studied, but the scenery whose influence I can trace most definitely throughout his works, varied as they are, is that of Yorkshire. Of all his drawings, I think, those of the Yorkshire series have the most heart in them, the most affectionate, simple, unwearied, serious finishing of truth. There is in them little seeking after effect, but a strong love of place; little exhibition of the artist's own powers or peculiarities, but intense appreciation of the smallest local minutia.'

The son of a London barber, Turner was born at Covent Garden on or around 23 April 1775. On reaching the age of fourteen he was admitted to the schools of the Royal Academy; at the age of twenty-four he became an Associate of the Royal Academy; at twenty-six he had progressed to a full Academician; and at thirty-two to Professor of Perspective. When he made his north-of-England tour at the close of the eighteenth century, the cult of the 'picturesque', popularized by the writings of the Reverend William Gilpin, was in vogue. Furthermore, as the 'Grand Tour' through Europe to Rome – an almost obligatory part of the education of the aristocracy and gentry of England – came to an end with the French revolutionary wars of the 1790s, it was suddenly fashionable for the wealthy and leisured to tour Britain instead, especially those areas renowned for their 'picturesque' scenery. Initially, the reason for travelling to the Continent was to learn about antiquities, art and culture, but most young bloods were lured away from these noble pursuits by less virtuous ones – novelty, amusement and pleasure. Turner's reason for travelling through the north of England, however, was to further his career. Indeed, after one of his paintings of Norham Castle 'took' (as he put it himself), he was never short of commissions. The person most influential in his rise from comparative obscurity to international fame was Edward Viscount Lascelles, eldest son of the 1st Earl of Harewood, and a wealthy patron of the arts. Preferring to commission young and up-and-coming artists, Lascelles invited Turner to his family home, Harewood House, near Leeds, in 1797. It was an opportunity and a privilege that the twenty-two-year-old barber's son was not prepared to miss.

King George III had been on the throne for thirty-seven years. His interest in the study of agriculture, which earned him the name 'Farmer George', coincided with dramatic improvements in farming methods brought about by such men as Thomas William Coke, 1st Earl of Leicester of the 2nd creation. Wealthy landowners also

began to erode the peasant farmer's traditional rights by enclosing their common fields: and, despite protests, Parliament passed around 1,500 private Enclosure Acts between the years 1760 and 1797. Nothing was going to stand in the way of the progress of the agricultural revolution, least of all the suffering of the poor.

In keeping with the prevailing trend, Arthur Young wrote *A Six Months Tour Through the North of England*. The book was first published in 1771, and it was essentially an account of the state of agriculture at the time, including recommendations for the improvement of 'waste lands'. Nevertheless, after visiting places like Fountains Abbey, Duncombe Park and York Minster, the Suffolk farmer sometimes strayed from his theme:

'I should apologise for introducing so many descriptions of houses, paintings, ornamented parks, lakes, &c. I am sensible they have little to do with agriculture, but there is, nevertheless, an utility in their being known.'

George III's preoccupation with the state of his health (he suffered from bouts of apparent madness – a condition that eventually became permanent) led to the development of seaside resorts such as Brighton, Lyme Regis and Scarborough. Having heard of the beneficial effects of seawater in 'diseases of the glands', the king started to bathe at Weymouth, thereby setting a new fashion. He also frequented Raven Hall (then a private residence, now a hotel), overlooking Robin Hood's Bay at Ravenscar.

But, above all else, the major change in England at the close of the eighteenth century was the arrival of the Industrial Revolution, the consequences of which were to transform the landscape and society of not only of Britain, but of the world. The shift was from a rural to an urban one: from most people living in the country to most living in towns; from goods being produced by hand to those being produced by machine. The greatest developments were in areas such as south Yorkshire where iron and large deposits of coal were to be found; or in west Yorkshire, where fast-running water was in plentiful supply to drive the machinery of the early textile mills. The inland transport of fuel, raw materials and finished goods was greatly improved by the development of the 'modern' canal network, which started with the construction of the Bridgewater Canal, the first section of which was opened in 1761. Built by James Brindley, it connected Manchester with the 3rd Duke of Bridgewater's coal mines at Worsley.

Despite the erection in 1779 of the world's first cast-iron bridge, at Ironbridge, Shropshire, and the starting in 1795 of Thomas Telford's cast-iron aqueduct, carrying the Llangollen Canal over the River Dee in North Wales, the state of the roads in northern England was little different to those in Celia Fiennes' time. A new system of turnpikes had been introduced after much violence and bloodshed, but in general most people avoided paying tolls by using alternative routes. Taking a turnpike, however, did not necessarily guarantee a road in good condition – as Arthur Young discovered:

'The turnpikes! as they have the assurance to call them; and the hardiness to make one pay for. From Chepstow to the half-way house between Newport hugeous holes as big as one's house, and abominable holes. The first six miles from Newport, they were so detestable, and without either direction-posts, or milestones, that I could not persuade myself I was on the turnpike, but had mistook the road.'

PEAK STEEL, RAVENSCAR

Established in 1970, the Ravenscar Trail – a three-mile, waymarked walk at Ravenscar – not only embraces some of the unique geological features and land forms of the headland, it also includes sites of historical interest (notably, the remains of alum works, considered to represent the best surviving example of England's first chemical industry). The Raven Hall Hotel, built as a private house in 1774, stands on the site of a Roman signal station. The cliffs, falling 600 feet to sea-level, display a complete sequence of strata, from the sandstone beds of the upper Ravenscar Group, at the top, to the grey Alum Shale of Upper Lias, on the shore. The block of resistant Middle Lias forming the prominent reef of Peak Steel was produced by a major geological fault.

'After admiring the portraits caught in a burst of sunlight by Adam-Salomon, the emotional sculptor who has given up painting, we no longer claim that photography is a trade – it is an art, it is more than an art, it is a solar phenomenon where the artist collaborates with the sun.'

Fox Talbot, likewise, saw photography as painting in another medium; a means of creating true and reliable images 'painted by Nature herself'. Unlike most of his contemporaries, however, he also realized that photography was not simply an art form, but a working tool: a means of recording and documenting information and images; a way of producing multiple reproductions of originals; a method of manipulating visual images; and a means of revealing a different view of the physical world than that experienced by the human eye.

Nevertheless, by the time Sutcliffe had acquired his first camera, the initial euphoria of photography as an art form was waning, and people were beginning to question its elevated status.

Sutcliffe, while never considering photography 'real art', always maintained that it was a form of creative expression in its own right. For him, it was not just a means of making a living; more importantly, it was an artistic method of capturing the effects of light and weather on the coastal landscape that he loved, which also included its people.

Born at Headingley, Leeds, on 6 October 1853, the son of the artist and art critic Thomas Sutcliffe, his fascination with the relatively new process led to a disastrous attempt to set up a photographic studio in Tunbridge Wells, Kent. In 1876, having been forced to sell the business because of mounting debts, he decided to return to the Yorkshire fishing port of Whitby (to which he and his parents had moved six years previously) and try again.

By profession he was a portrait photographer, but his atmospheric and beautifully composed studies of the people, harbour and ships of Whitby sold well to the tourist trade. In 1886, probably the most famous of his monochrome pictures, *The Water Rats* (a scene of naked boys playing on boats in Whitby harbour) was shown at the annual exhibition of the Royal Photographic Society. It so impressed the Prince of Wales (later King Edward VII) that he ordered a large print of the scene to hang in his London home, Marlborough House. Whether the prince knew or cared that Sutcliffe (as he himself claimed) had been excommunicated by the clergy of Whitby for 'exhibiting such an indecent print in his shopwindow to the corruption of the young of the other sex' is not known.

At the close of the nineteenth century, travel was no longer the privilege of the upper classes, as the arrival of the railway had opened up the coast and countryside to the working- and lower-middle-class inhabitants of the industrial cities and towns. Tourism was now available to the masses.

The world's first permanent public railway to use steam locomotion was the Stockton and Darlington, opened in 1825. Five years later, the Liverpool and Manchester railway inaugurated the first regular steam

NORTH YORKSHIRE MOORS RAILWAY, NEWTON DALE

The twenty-four-mile Pickering-to-Whitby railway line, designed by George Stephenson, was officially opened as a horse-drawn carriageway on 26 May 1836. From the market town of Pickering, the route went north through Newton Dale, Goathland and Beck Hole to Grosmont; from where it followed the Esk Valley eastward to Whitby port. At Beck Hole the incline was so steep that coaches had to be hauled up by rope. Between 1845 and 1847 George Hudson, 'the Railway King', converted the line to take steam locomotives. So sharp were some of the bends, however, that it was jokingly said that churns of milk loaded at Whitby contained butter when they reached Pickering. The line closed in 1965, but the section between Grosmont and Pickering was reopened by the N.Y.M.H.R. Trust in 1973.

'LIMESTONE COUNTRY', NEAR SETTLE

On his way to Gordale Scar in 1769, Thomas Gray travelled through the limestone country of Craven in the north-west corner of Yorkshire: 'The nipping air, tho' the afternoon was growing very bright, now taught us we were in Craven, the road was all up and down, though nowhere very steep; to the left were the mountain tops, to the right a wide valley, all inclosed ground, and beyond it high hills again. In approaching Settle, the crags on the left drew nearer to our way, till we descended Brunton-brow into a cheerful valley (though thin of trees) to Giggleswick, a village with a small piece of water by its side, covered with cots.' Returning from Gordale, he summed up his impressions: 'Craven, after all, is an unpleasing country when seen from a height.'

WHITBY HARBOUR

As the number of ships wrecked off the stormy Yorkshire coast since the start of the sixteenth century is probably in excess of 50,000, it is not surprising that Bram Stoker's fictional Russian schooner (carrying Dracula, in the form of a black dog) should be driven aground at Whitby: 'on that accumulation of sand and gravel washed by many tides and many storms into the south-east corner of the pier jutting under the East Cliff, known locally as Tate Hill Pier. It so happened that there was no one at the moment on Tate Hill Pier, as all those whose houses are in close proximity were either in bed or were out on the heights above.' When the coastguard eventually climbed on board he found a corpse lashed to the wheel with a crucifix fastened by a set of beads around both wrists.

passenger service. Yet, it was not until 1847 that the first steam train pulled into the station at Whitby. Other methods of transport inevitably suffered as a result. The rush and excitement of establishing a new railway network throughout the island diverted funds away from the canals (which gradually fell into disuse) and brought an end to the turnpikes. At their peak, the turnpikes amounted to an impressive total of more than 30,000 miles of toll road.

For centuries, Whitby's isolated position on the far side of the North York Moors meant that it was easier to approach from the sea than from the land. Most of its trade and communication with the outside world was, therefore, by way of sailing vessels or steam ships. Following the opening of the railway, the port suffered a sharp decline – counteracted only by an increase in the number of summer visitors to the town.

Yet, if Sutcliffe's photographs are anything to go by, the state of most of the country roads in north-east Yorkshire showed little improvement, and most of the traffic on them remained the horse or the horse-drawn cart. In marked contrast, most of the streets in Whitby were cobbled. The former turnpikes, of course, had been greatly improved due to financial incentives. Among those who profited from building new roads were John Metcalf (Blind Jack of Knaresborough), Thomas Telford and John Loudon McAdam. Yet, despite Blind Jack's construction of better main roads through the nearby Vale of York, the routes across the North York Moors still remained little more than tracks.

Interestingly, in 1873, Sutcliffe was commissioned by John Ruskin to photograph his house and garden at Brantwood, overlooking Coniston Water. The fragile glass-plate negatives managed to survive the hazardous journey from the Lake District to Tunbridge Wells. But nearly all of the photographer's early work was broken during the move to Whitby. Since Sutcliffe's photographic equipment was heavy, cumbersome and extremely fragile, coupled with the fact that he was not particularly strong, it is hardly surprising that he chose to work almost exclusively in and around his home port, seldom straying inland further than the Esk valley, and only rarely up on to the high and rugged moors. In the *Yorkshire Weekly Post* of 8 October 1910, he wrote:

'After carrying one's apparatus for even the short eight hours of an Autumn day one feels "dogtired" by evening. Weighed at the scales the apparatus does not weigh much, only two stones four-and-a-half pounds . . . To be sure, many amateur photographers in the 'sixties used to carry double this weight; before dryplates came in we had the darktent, silver bath, developers, fixers, and water bottle to carry as well.'

SAND HILL & COMMONDALE

In *Forty Years in a Moorland Parish*, the Reverend Atkinson told the story of one Commondale farmer's attempt to stop a witch (in the form of a hare) from stealing the milk from his cows by night. As the cows of the village community were usually all pastured together in one common field, the real culprit was often a dishonest neighbour. However, 'many cases of apparently mysterious failure of milk would be referred to the witch'. Determined to catch the witch-hare in the act and shoot it – 'not with leaden pellets, but with silver slugs' – the farmer concealed himself in the field. When the creature eventually appeared, with glaring eyes as big as saucers, fear and superstition turned to panic, causing the farmer to throw away his gun and flee in horrified terror.

In those pioneering years, as with other 'travel' photographers, Sutcliffe had to carry everything necessary to produce and fix a photographic image, including a portable darkroom. Roger Fenton, who was the founder of The Photographic Society in 1853 (later to become The Royal Photographic Society), transported his apparatus inside a horse-drawn 'Photographic Van'. After Fenton's retirement from professional photography in 1861, his equipment was purchased by Francis Frith, who, having just returned from his third tour of the Middle East, set up a photographic company to produce tourist views of the British Isles. In Egypt, Frith carried his bulky photographic paraphernalia in a specially constructed wickerwork carriage, which also doubled as a darkroom.

Among Frith's photographs of England are several taken in Whitby, including a little barefoot girl standing on the harbour quay – a subject clearly revealing the influence of his illustrious contemporary, Frank Meadow Sutcliffe. Indeed, Sutcliffe, at the beginning of his photographic career, was commissioned by Frith to take a series of views of Yorkshire abbeys and castles. Frith also gave him a mahogany Kinnear camera. However, it had one irritating disadvantage (which was probably why Frith gave it away) – the position of the focusing handle, which Sutcliffe related had been placed there 'for the sole purpose of pulling the hairs out of my beard each time I use this infernal machine'.

Nevertheless, despite many such hindrances, Sutcliffe's photographs won more than sixty gold, silver and bronze medals at exhibitions all over the world. In *Photography* (31 May 1894) he wrote:

'The student in search of the picturesque will soon find that the beauty of a subject depends more on the condition under which it is seen than the material of which it is composed, and often the less material there is the better the chance of success.'

In 1923, after retiring from professional photography, Sutcliffe became curator of Whitby Museum, a post that he held until a month or so before his death on 31 May 1941, aged eighty-eight. Albeit belatedly, in recognition of his great pioneering contribution to the art of photography, he was made an Honorary Fellow of the Royal Photographic Society in 1935.

Today, his monochrome views of the ancient port of Whitby stir memories and emotions of a 'great' and vanished time – when Victoria ruled an empire, when huge areas of the world map were coloured red, and when Britain, emphatically, 'ruled the ocean waves'.

GREAT FRYUP DALE, FROM GLAISDALE MOOR

Running parallel to each other, east of Danby Dale, are the two farming dales of Great and Little Fryup. Both have streams (appropriately called Great Fryup Beck and Little Fryup Beck); both of which are tributaries of the River Esk. The name 'Fryup' is thought to be derived from 'Friga', an Old English personal name, and 'up' or 'hop' meaning 'a valley'. The place where the Fryups meet is known as Fairy Cross Plain. An elderly parishioner told the Rev. Atkinson that it was so called because just in front of the Ship Inn (now a private house) 'two ways or roads used to cross, and that gave the 'cross' part of the name. And as to the rest of it, or the name 'Fairy', everybody knew that years and years ago the fairies had 'a desper't haunt o'thae hill-ends just ahint the Public'.'

In 1997, Rob Talbot travelled through Yorkshire recording his impressions on two robust and extremely portable cameras – a Nikon and a Hasselblad. Unlike Fiennes, Turner and Sutcliffe, however, he had unlimited access to a road and motorway network that could take him to any part of the island in hours, rather than days or weeks.

Since the close of the Victorian age, technological progress had advanced to an astonishing degree, almost beyond the wildest dreams of such 'scientific' visionaries as H. G. Wells and Jules Verne. Man had not only explored almost every part of the planet, he had gone to the moon and come back. Even more incredibly, at the very same time that he was 240,000 miles away in space he had transmitted visual and audio signals that were seen and heard almost instantaneously by millions of people on Earth. Further still, the traditional optical-mechanical technology for recording images had advanced from chemical processes to electronic ones.

HELMSLEY CASTLE

Strategically situated on an outcrop of rock on the north bank of the River Rye, immediately west of the market town of Helmsley, the ruins of the castle date from the end of the twelfth century, when Robert de Roos was lord of the manor. Although there is no evidence of a motte-and-bailey (typical of early Norman castles), it is thought that the former Lord of Helmsley, Walter l'Espec, built some form of stone stronghold on the site. (He died in 1154, and was founder of Rievaulx Abbey and Kirkham Priory). Although the keep and curtain walls date from the time of de Roos, the barbican, guarding the main entrance, was built in the mid-thirteenth century. In 1644, after a three-month siege, the castle was left in ruins. The property is now in the care of English Heritage.

In 1997, however, Talbot was still using the traditional method of photography. Born in Coventry on 23 January 1958, he embarked on a career as a professional photographer in his late teens. From the formation of the Talbot and Whiteman partnership in 1985 he has taken in excess of 50,000 photographs, and produced some twenty illustrated books covering almost every region of England.

When visiting an area for the first time, Talbot's priority is to discover the qualities and peculiarities that make it special and unique. This is invariably dictated by the geology – the underlying rock that gives the scenery its own distinctive character and form. After all, despite humanity's 10,000-year contribution to its surface appearance, today's landscape is essentially the product of many millions of years of natural evolution and

the relentless effects of the elements.

As can be seen from the photographs in this book, the Yorkshire landscape is incredibly rich and varied. Its rocks reveal evidence of a 500-million-year journey, not only through time, but across the surface of the planet from far south of the equator to its present position in the north. Nor has the journey stopped!

During this epic voyage, that patch of the Earth's crust that was to become Yorkshire underwent cataclysmic upheavals and extreme climatic changes. The oldest rocks date from the time

when Yorkshire lay under the sea in the southern hemisphere. These old ocean bed rocks, in the form of slates, sandstones and shales, can be seen in the area around Malham and Ingle-

ton, especially in the cliff at Thornton Force. The block of limestone above the slate is mainly composed of the crushed shells and skeletons of primitive sea organisms, laid down when much of the Dales were covered by a shallow tropical lagoon.

In addition to identifying the type of rock that characterizes an area, Talbot also studies the signs of human activity in the landscape: the use of local stone in buildings and monuments, for example; the changes brought about by industry, commerce and farming; the consequences of developments in communications and trade; and the effect on the countryside of the explosion in tourism, coupled with attempts by conservation bodies to 'protect, maintain and enhance' the 'natural' scenery.

On 5 August 1993 the *British Journal of Photography* published a major feature on the Talbot and Whiteman partnership, under the heading 'A Country Practice'. In it, Talbot was asked if his photographs were little more than 'a glossy manipulation of the land?':

'We are not about documentary photography; our work is unashamedly promotional. If I see some rubbish lying on the ground, I am going to clear it up before I take a picture. A documentary photographer would shoot the image as a story on man ruining the environment.'

With regard to the technical aspects of photography, Talbot is tight-lipped. For him, the camera is merely a tool. The only difference between his expensive cameras, and those that are less expensive, but more sophisticated, is their robust construction, enabling them to withstand the knocks and bangs of constant use. 'What is all important,' he maintains, 'is the scene, the light, the mood, the seasons and the composition.'

THORNTON FORCE, NEAR INGLETON

Since the latter half of the eighteenth century, the waterfalls and caves around Ingleton have been popular with tourists. Thornton Force – with a drop of forty-six feet – can be reached by way of a four-mile, circular walk through the valleys of the Doe and Twiss, which starts at Ingleton and follows a route that was first opened to the public in 1885. In terms of geology, the trail reveals the ancient basement rocks of the Pennines, crosses three major faults, and, at Thornton Force, presents a classic example of 'unconformity' (an abrupt change or break between rocks of a vastly different age). Above the 'unconformity', the cliff consists of horizontal layers of Carboniferous limestone, while below are almost vertical layers of older Ordovician slate.

Grassholme Res.
Grassholme
Selset Res.
Lunedale
Romaldkirk
Cotherstone
Balderhead Res.
Baldersdale
Hury Res.
Barnard Castle
Brough
Bowes
Egglestone Abbey

Redcar
Saltburn-by-the-Sea
Boulby
Staithes
Middlesbrough
Port Mulgrave
Ormesby
Loftus
Kettleness
Marton
Guisborough
Runswick Bay
Lythe
Sandsend
Yarm
Roseberry Topping
Wayworth Moor
Mulgrave Castle
Whitby
Great Ayton
Commondale
Kildale
Lealholm
CLEVELAND RAIN
Danby
Ingleby Greenhow
Castleton
Glaisdale
Egton
Little Beck
Robin's Hood Bay
Westerdale
Little Fryup
Grosmont
Rave

△ Tan Hill
YORKSHIRE DALES
NORTH RIDING
Beck Hole
Langthwaite
Mount Grace Priory
Danby High Moor
Goathland
West Stonesdale
Pry Hill
Richmond
Cleveland Hills
Farndale Moor
Saltergate Moor
Fylingdales Moor
ARKENGARTHDALE
Easby
Osmotherly
Bransdale
N. YORK MOORS
Keld
Ivelet
Reeth
Grinton
Bilsdey Ridge
Rosedale Abbey
Grime Moor
Thwaite
Gunnerside
Northallerton
East Moors
Spaunton Moor
Newton Dale
Muker
Oxnop
SWALEDALE
Howgill
Hambleton Hills
Gillamoor
Lastingham
Levisham
Butter Tubs Pass
Castle Bolton
Redmire
Leyburn
Bedale
Hutton-le-Hole
Sedbergh
Hardraw
Askrigg
Sutton Bank
Rievaulx Abbey
Kirkdale
Kirkbymoorside
Scarboro
Hawes
Bainbridge
Aysgarth
Middleham
Thirsk
Helmsley
Pickering
Thornton-le-Dale
Cowgill
Semer Water
WENSLEYDALE
Jervaulx Abbey
Kilburn
Duncombe Park
Dent
BISHOPDALE
Coxwold
Byland Abbey
Ampleforth
R. Derwent
Whernside △
LANGSTROTHDALE
Masham
Newburgh
Slingsby
Ribblehead Viaduct
Yockenthwaite
Ilton
R. Ure
VALE OF PICKERING
Malton
Settrington
Chapel-le-Dale
Hubberholme
Easingwold
Dalby
Castle Howard
Ingleborough △
Litton
Studley Royal
Ripon
Boroughbridge
Sheriff Hutton
Kirkham Priory
Wharram Percy
Ingleton
Pen-Y-Ghent △
LITTONDALE
Kettlewell
NIDDERDALE
Fountains Abbey
Clapham
Hornton-in-Ribblesdale
Arncliffe
Brimham Rocks
Great Drif
Austwick
Malham Moor
Kilnsey
Pateley Bridge
VALE OF YORK
Little Driffield
Stainforth
Malham Tarn
Grassington
Ripley
Giggleswick
Settle
Linton
Burnsall
Knaresborough
Kirkby Malham
Appletreewick
Harrogate
YORK
WOLDS
EAST RIDIN
Slaidburn
Bolton Abbey
R. Derwent
Skipton
Pocklington
Earby
Ilkley
Harewood
Tadcaster
Cowling
Wainman's Pinnacle
WEST RIDING
Market Weighton
Keighley
Bev
Haworth
Kirkstall
Oxenhope
LEEDS
Top Withens
Bradford
Selby
R. Ouse
M62
Heptonstall
Hebden Bridge
Goole
Stoodley Pike
Batley
Castleford
Todmorden
Halifax
Pontefract
M62
Blackstone Edge
Dewsbury
Wakefield
M18
Huddersfield
M1
Marsden
Holmfirth
Barnsley
Hinchliffe Mill
Doncaster
R. Trent
M180
Rotherham
M18
Loxley
Stanage Edge
SHEFFIELD
Hathersage
Hathersage Moor
A1(M)
M1
Dronfield

PENNINES

R. Swale

Bidsey Ridge

A1(M)

R. Aire

R. Ouse

● Town or villag

○ Photographic site

△ Mountain peak

N O R T H

S E A

Filey

Bempton Cliffs

Flamborough Head

n   Boynton

Bridlington

n Agnes

Hornsea

Mappleton

H O L D E R N E S S

GSTON-UPON-HULL

Withernsea

H u m b e r

Grimsby

In 2097, some one hundred years hence . . . Who knows? Just as today's technological developments would certainly astonish the Victorians, tomorrow's will certainly astonish us. Perhaps those who travel through Yorkshire may no longer need to record their impressions on any kind of material or device. They may not even have to set foot on Yorkshire soil, breathe Yorkshire air, or experience Yorkshire weather. Instead, their journey may take place in some type of computer-generated three-dimensional landscape – in a Yorkshire of 'virtual reality'.

Even now, as I write, the storage of video and sound recordings of the Yorkshire Dales on a central electronic database is under serious consideration, if not actually underway. As the *Observer* of 17 March 1996 reported, under the heading 'Take a seat and walk the Dales':

'Climb every mountain, ford every stream, follow every rainbow till you find your dream – all without stirring from your armchair. That is the promise that may soon come true for lovers of the Yorkshire Dales.'

As the canal network gave way to that of the railway, and the railway to that of the motorway, perhaps the motorway network will give way to mass-travel by air. Then, maybe, travellers through the 'real' Yorkshire countryside will find themselves alone (except possibly for the locals) in a landscape more reminiscent of 1697 than 1997.

That is, unless they happen to look up!

A Tour Through the Ridings

'The whole shire is divided into three parts,
which according to three-quarters of the world
are called The West-Riding, The East-Riding, and
The North-Riding. West-Riding, for a good while
is compassed in with the River Ouse, with the
bound of Lancashire, and with the south limits
of the shire, and beareth towards the west and
south. East-Riding, looketh to the sun-rising
and the ocean, which together with the River
Derwent incloseth it. North-Rising reacheth
northward, hemmed in, as it were, with the
River Tees, with Derwent, and a long race of the
River Ouse. In that West part, out of the western
mountains or hills in the confines, issue many
rivers which Ouse alone, entertaineth every one
and carrieth them all with him unto Humber.'

Britannia

WILLIAM CAMDEN

HIGGER TOR, HATHERSAGE MOOR

On the craggy, boulder-strewn moorlands, south-west of Sheffield and close to the Derbyshire border, is a prominent gritstone outcrop known as Higger Tor, reaching some 1,400 feet above sea-level. 'Higger', sometimes spelled 'Higgar', is thought to be a corruption of 'higher'. Nearby, standing on a lower height of gritstone, are the remains of Carl Wark, an ancient and enigmatic fortress thought by some to date from the Iron Age, and by others from the Romano-British period or even post-Roman (Dark Age) times. To the north-east, in Yorkshire, is Burbage Rocks, one of a series of long gritstone 'edges' that extend for several miles along the eastern side of the Derbyshire Peak District. Part of the boundary between Yorkshire and Derbyshire runs along Stanage Edge.

HINCHLIFFE MILL

Although the settlements along the Holme Valley have benefited considerably from the fast-flowing streams and rivers of the surrounding moorlands, especially with regard to the textile industry, there have been several occasions when floods have caused immense damage and tragic loss of life. The worst was in 1852, when heavy rain caused the Bilberry Reservoir to burst its dam, releasing a vast, destructive torrent of water down the valley. At the woollen-weaving village of Hinchliffe Mill, near Holmfirth, six three-storey houses on the river bank – built to accommodate the weavers' looms on the upper floor – were washed away. Of their forty-two occupants, only seven were saved. So great was the damage to the mills and their machinery, that almost 6,000 people lost their work.

HOLMFIRTH

In the Holme Valley, south-west of Huddersfield, the Pennine textile town of Holmfirth is noted for being the centre of 'Summer Wine Country' – the area where the BBC set their long-running television comedy series *Last of the Summer Wine*. Holy Trinity Church, often featured in the series, was built after the previous church was severely damaged in the flood of 1777. Up the steps behind the church can be found the old lock-up known locally as 'T'owd Towser'. Dating from 1597, it is reputedly the oldest building in the town. The monument, known as 'T'owd Genn', was erected in 1801 to mark the 'Peace of Amiens', the fourteen-month interlude in Britain's war with France. It was during this welcome respite that Holmfirth's valuable overseas markets for cloth were briefly restored.

HEBDEN BRIDGE

At the confluence of the rivers Calder and Hebden, this old mill town takes its name from the packhorse bridge that spanned the Hebden in medieval times. The present bridge dates from about 1510. Even before the town was transformed by developments relating to the Industrial Revolution, it was a busy centre of the woollen industry, with cloth being woven on hand-looms in homes. Its position, amid the sheep-rearing Pennine uplands, ensured an abundance of wool. The domestic industry, however, was ruined by the mechanization of the cloth-making process and its centralization in factories. Shortage of space in the steep-sided valley led to the building of four-storey terraced houses (in reality, rows of two-storeyed houses built one above the other).

STOODLEY PIKE, NEAR TODMORDEN

Situated on the Pennine Way, almost 1,300 feet above sea-level and some two miles east of the market town of Todmorden, the 120-feet-high obelisk of Stoodley Pike was erected to commemorate the first Peace Treaty of Paris and the abdication of Napoleon in 1814. After Napoleon's escape from Elba, however, work on the construction of the monument was suspended. It was resumed when the French Emperor was finally defeated at Waterloo on 18 June 1815. By then, coincidentally, the Treaty of Ghent had also brought peace between Britain and the United States of America. In 1854, the monument collapsed and was rebuilt. The same happened in 1919. A door at its base leads up a dark, winding stairway to a platform some forty feet up, with views over the Calder valley and the surrounding moors.

TOP WITHENS, HAWORTH MOOR

After the deaths of Emily and Anne, Charlotte Brontë wrote: 'I am free to walk on the moors; but when I go out there alone, everything reminds me of the times when others were with me, and then the moors seem a wilderness, featureless, solitary, saddening. My sister Emily had a particular love for them, and there is not a knoll of heather, not a branch of fern, not a young bilberry leaf, not a fluttering lark or linnet, but reminds me of her. The distant prospects were Anne's delight, and when I look round, she is in the blue tints, the pale mists, the waves and shadows of the horizon. In the hill-country silence, their poetry comes by lines and stanzas into my mind . . .' Top Withens farmhouse, which is now only a ruin, is popularly believed to have been the inspiration for Emily's famous work *Wuthering Heights*.

HAWORTH PARSONAGE

Overlooking the bleak church-yard of St Michael and All Angels, Haworth is the world-famous parsonage that was the home of the Brontë sisters – Charlotte, Emily and Anne – for the greater part of their tragically short and isolated lives. Although they were born at Thornton (near Bradford) in April 1816, July 1818 and January 1820 respectively, the three sisters moved to Haworth in June 1820, after their Irish-born father, the Reverend Patrick Brontë, had been appointed perpetual curate of the parish. He outlived them all. Their mother, Maria, died in 1821, followed four years later by their two sisters Maria and Elizabeth. Branwell, their only brother, died a drug addict in 1848. Emily died a few months later; Anne in 1849; and Charlotte in 1855. Haworth Parsonage is now the Brontë Museum.

WAINMAN'S PINNACLE, NEAR COWLING

On the gritstone escarpment of Earl Crag, overlooking the Colne to Keighley road, near Ickornshaw and Cowling, are two stone-built monuments – Wainman's Pinnacle and Lund's Tower – both conspicuous landmarks for miles around. Nicknamed, respectively, the 'Cowling Pepper Pot' and 'Sutton Salt Pot', their origins have long been a subject of local controversy. The former (subsequently rebuilt) is said to have been erected by Richard Bradley Wainman, of Carr Head Hall, either to commemorate the defeat of Napoleon or in memory of his son who was killed at the Battle of Waterloo in 1815. The latter was built by James Lund of Malsis Hall, either to commemorate the twenty-first birthday of his daughter, Ethel, or Queen Victoria's Diamond Jubilee of 1897.

THE TERRACE, HAREWOOD HOUSE

Set in 1,000 acres of 'Capability' Brown parkland, Harewood House has been the home of the Lascelles family since 1738, when Henry Lascelles – a wealthy Barbados sugar plantation owner – purchased the estate. It was then centred on the house at Gawthorpe. In 1759, his son, Edwin, 1st Lord Harewood, started to build a new house on the present hill-top site. The building was designed by John Carr and its interiors by Robert Adam. In 1843 Sir Charles Barry remodelled the house externally and added the Terrace. The house is also noted for being the home of HRH The Princess Royal, daughter of King George V, who married Henry, 6th Earl of Harewood, in 1922.

BOLTON PRIORY, BOLTON ABBEY

Standing on the west bank of the River Wharfe, near the ancient village of Bolton Abbey, are the remains of a priory founded for Augustinian canons from Embsay, near Skipton, in 1154. The house was originally founded in 1120 by Cecily, the wife of William Meschin and the daughter of Robert de Romille (or Rumilly), the first Norman lord of Bolton. It was through the benevolence of Cecily's daughter, Alice, that the canons were able to move to the more favourable site at Bolton. Tradition says that Alice founded the priory to commemorate the death of her son, the 'Boy of Egremont', who was drowned while trying to cross the Strid. Records, however, reveal that he was still alive at the foundation. The priory ruins are reputedly haunted by ghostly monks dressed in black.

The Strid,
near Bolton Abbey

In *Visits to Remarkable Places* (1890), William Howitt visited the ruined priory at Bolton Abbey, and also the Strid, some two miles upstream. 'The Strid is not so much a waterfall as a narrow passage torn by the river [Wharfe] through its bed of solid rock, through which it rushes with tremendous fury and a stunning din. Many people, who go expecting to see a sheer cascade, are at first disappointed; but no one can stand long by it without feeling a sense of its power and savage grandeur grow upon him. It is indeed a place "most tempting to bestride;" but narrow as the opening appears, its real width is much greater than its apparent one; and very dangerous, both on that account and from the slipperiness of the rocks. One slip of the foot, and the leap is into eternity.'

UPPER WHARFEDALE, NEAR KETTLEWELL

Around the former textile and lead-mining village of Kettlewell, with its grey-stone cottages and houses, the level, glacier-moulded valley of the River Wharfe rises – through lush pastures, criss-crossed by miles of walling – to steep, scree-sloped limestone cliffs. Kilnsey Crag, three miles south of the village, is an enormous cliff of Great Scar Limestone, 170 feet high. Because of its forty-feet overhang – created during the Ice Age by the grinding action of the Wharfedale glacier – it presents rock climbers with a formidable challenge. Turner sketched the crag and surrounding landscape during his tour of 1816. By drawing everything in meticulous detail, he engraved each scene on his memory and, thereby, was able to recall specific moments of the tour at a later date.

WHARFEDALE, FROM LITTLE HUNTERS SLEETS

'Out of the foot of Craven-hills springs the river Wharfe,' wrote William Camden (1551–1623) in *Britannia*, after visiting Wharfedale. 'If any one would derive the name of it from a British word Guer, swift, the nature of the river will favour him; for its course is swift and violent, fretful and angry, as it were, at those stones which obstruct its passage; and so rolls them along very strangely, especially when it swells by a wet winter. However, it is dangerous and rapid even in the summer time; as I am sensible by experience, who in my travels this way run no small risk in passing it. For it has either such slippery stones, that a horse's foot cannot fix in them; or else the current itself is so strong, that it drives them from under his feet.'

YOCKENTHWAITE FARM, LANGSTROTHDALE

In Langstrothdale, the name given to upper Wharfedale, above Buckden, are several small farming hamlets that owe their origins to Scandinavian settlers. The name 'Yockenthwaite' is Norse rather than Danish, and means 'Eogan's woodland clearing'. In most instances, the Danes entered Yorkshire from the east, and the Norsemen from the west by way of Cumbria and Lancashire. Many of the Noresmen were descendants of Norwegians who had settled in Ireland, hence the Irish personal name in 'Yockenthwaite'. 'Hubberholme', which is found further down Langstrothdale, is thought to derive its name from 'Hubba' – a ninth-century Norse chieftain. Places with the suffix -by (such as Whitby, Easby and Carperby) and -thorpe are fairly positive indicators of a former Danish settlement.

RIVER WHARFE, LANGSTROTHDALE

After devastating and depopulating vast areas of the Yorkshire countryside in his determination to remove, once and for all, the threat to Norman rule in England from the insurgent people of the north, William the Conqueror rewarded his supporters with generous parcels of land. Large tracts of the Dales, not necessarily wooded, became the exclusive hunting preserve of the new Norman nobility, with severe penalties for anyone caught poaching the 'protected' game. The lords of Skipton hunted in Littondale and Langstrothdale Chase; the lords of Middleham in Wensleydale Forest and Bishopdale Chase; and the lords of Richmond in Swaledale and Arkengarthdale Forest. Today, much of upper Langstrothdale has been planted with conifer trees by the Forestry Commission.

LITTONDALE, FROM HESLEDEN BERGH

Charles Kingsley based 'Vendale' in *The Water Babies* (1863) on Littondale: 'A quiet, silent, rich, happy place; a narrow crack cut deep into the earth; so deep, and so out of the way, that the bad bogies can hardly find it out and if you want to see it for yourself, you must go up into the High Craven, and search from Bolland Forest north by Ingleborough, to the Nine Standards and Cross Fell; and if you have not found it, you must turn south, and search the Lake Mountains, down to Scaw Fell and the sea; and then, if you have not found it, you must go northward again by merry Carlisle, and search the Cheviots all across . . . then, whether you have found Vendale or not, you will have found such a country, and such a people, as ought to make you proud of being a British boy.'

WATLOWES DRY VALLEY, MALHAM COVE

The major east–west fracture, known as the Mid-Craven Fault, was caused millions of years ago by a massive upheaval in the earth's crust, in which the rocks to the south slipped and dropped vertically to reveal the 300-feet-high cliff face of Malham Cove. Above the cove, the steep-sided Watlowes Dry Valley was essentially formed by Ice Age meltwater coming from the direction of Malham Tarn, pouring down the valley and over the lip of the cove in a spectacular waterfall, higher than Niagara. Although Watlowes no longer has a river running overground through it, the Malham Beck emerges from a crack at the base of the cove. This water comes from a stream that sinks underground near Smelt Mill Chimney, some one and a half miles north-west of Watlowes.

MALHAM MOOR, NEAR MALHAM TARN

The limestone plateau of Malham Moor, between the Mid-Craven Fault and the North Craven Fault, was drained in ancient times by streams that ran overground, but which now run underground, leaving dry river beds and dry waterfalls on the surface. One such stream, the source of the River Aire, rises on Malham Tarn, disappears underground at Water Sinks, north of Watlowes, and re-emerges at Aire Head Springs, just south of Malham village (not at the foot of Malham Cove, as is often thought). Although Malham Tarn lies in the heart of limestone country, its bed is formed of boulder clay resting on impervious Silurian slate (which was brought near the surface by the geological upheaval of the North Craven Fault). It is a natural lake, formed when the valley was blocked by a glacial moraine.

MALHAM, FROM MALHAM COVE

From the deeply fissured limestone pavement at the top of Malham Cove are extensive views of the surrounding moorland, including the village of Malham itself. Although the oldest houses in Malham date mainly from the seventeenth and eighteenth centuries, the village itself was founded long before – possibly as early as the mid seventh century. The derivation of the name 'Malham' is uncertain: some suggest that it is of Old English origin; others suggest Old Norse. Evidence of prehistoric occupation, notably Iron Age enclosures, can be found in the vicinity. During medieval times, nearly all of the land around Malham was farmed either by Bolton Priory or Fountains Abbey. Today most of the area is still farmed, including the high limestone grasslands.

MALHAM COVE

Whilst staying at Tarn House, on the north shore of Malham Tarn, Charles Kingsley reputedly asked one of his fellow guests to explain the dark streaks on the curved limestone crag of Malham Cove. From the jesting reply – that they were made by a chimney sweep sliding down the cliff – he was inspired to write *The Water Babies*. Having run away from his master, Mr Grimes, Tom found himself at the top of a high cliff: 'He did not know that it was three hundred feet below. You would have been giddy, perhaps, at looking down: but Tom was not. He was a brave little chimney sweep; and when he found himself on the top of a high cliff . . . down he went . . . But of course, he dirtied everything terribly as he went. There has been a great black smudge all down the crag ever since.'

SHORKLEY HILL, MALHAM

The public footpath, from the curved limestone crag of Malham Cove to the secluded waterfall of Janet's Foss and the dramatic gorge of Gordale Scar, passes the hillside pastures of Shorkley Hill, where traces of earlier, Iron Age field systems can also be found. During medieval times, the increased demand for more arable land in the area forced farmers to exploit the unploughed pastureland higher up the hillsides, above the more fertile valley floors and sides. On these slopes, often steep, they gradually created, with the plough, a stepped series of long terraces. At Malham, these strip lynchets probably remained in productive use until the fields were enclosed in the late eighteenth century. Although they are now grassed over, the terraces can still be discerned on the hillside.

GORDALE SCAR, NEAR MALHAM

In 1769 Thomas Gray visited the deep, narrowing, limestone gorge of Gordale Scar. Venturing to within twelve feet of the waterfall, he described the 'horror of the place' in a letter to his friend, Dr Wharton: 'in one part of its top, more exposed to the weather, there are loose stones that hang in the air, and threaten visibly some idle spectator with instant destruction. It is safer to shelter yourself close to its bottom, and trust to the mercy of that enormous mass, which nothing but an earthquake can stir. The gloomy uncomfortable day well suited the savage aspect of the place, and made it still more formidable. I stayed there, not without shuddering, a quarter of an hour, and thought my trouble richly paid; for the impression will last for life.'

THORNTON FORCE, NEAR INGLETON

In *Modern Painters*, Ruskin wrote: 'Turner was the only painter who had ever represented the surface of calm or the force of agitated water. He obtains this expression of force . . . by fearless and full rendering of its forms. He never loses himself and his subject in the splash of the fall, his presence of mind never fails as he goes down; he does not blind us with the spray, or veil the countenance of his fall with its own drapery. A little crumbling white, or lightly rubbed paper, will soon give the effect of indiscriminate foam; but nature gives more than foam, she shows beneath it, and through it, a peculiar character of exquisitely studied form bestowed on every wave and line of fall; and it is this variety of definite character which Turner always aims at.'

ST JAMES CHURCH, CLAPHAM

Nestling in a wooded valley at the south-eastern foot of Ingleborough, the village of Clapham dates mainly from the 1760s, when Oliver Farrer, a wealthy lawyer, purchased the estate. Some sixty years later, the Farrers built Ingleborough Hall, and enlarged the village by the addition of new houses. Many of the old houses were also rebuilt. The church of St James, with its Perpendicular tower, is mostly nineteenth century. The old smithy was once the home of Joseph, the father of Michael Faraday (1791–1867), the discoverer of electro-magnetism. One of the estate owners was Reginald Farrer (1880–1920), the 'Father of English rock gardening', who introduced many rare and exotic plants to Britain. The nature trail named after him leads from the village to Ingleborough Cave.

NORBER BOULDERS, NEAR AUSTWICK

At Norber Brow, on the flanks of Ingleborough and some 500 feet above the village of Austwick, the limestone plateau is strewn with hundreds of giant boulders, or 'erratics'. The reason for their presence in the landscape remained unexplained for many years; for the older Silurian stone is usually found beneath the younger Carboniferous limestone, not above it. Geologists now know that each boulder, weighing several tons, was transported from Crummack Dale – about half a mile away – by a retreating Ice Age glacier. The reason that many of the 'erratics' are perched on isolated plinths, is due to the fact that the surrounding softer limestone – unprotected by the umbrella effect of the harder boulder – has been dissolved away by rainwater over thousands of years.

INGLEBOROUGH, FROM SOUTHER SCALES

In 1898 Lewis Moore warned of the dangers of 'speleology' around Ingleborough: 'This sport has been called mountaineering reversed, cave hunting, potholing, and, by Philistines, mouldy warping. Its pursuers have dignified it with the more scientific name, speleology. Its pleasures are more real than apparent, and, when seeking them, it is wise to remember the rules of the game. The greater pot holes should not, and probably will not, be attempted without an adequate supply of the necessary tackle, and the assistance of a strong party. It is the less obvious dangers of the smaller ones which call for a few words of caution . . . Small things they may be in themselves, but they contain possibilities of serious peril to a solitary explorer or a weak party.'

INGLEBOROUGH, FROM SCALES MOOR

In *Modern Painters*, first published in five volumes between 1834 and 1860, John Ruskin wrote: 'I have been often at great heights in the Alps in rough weather, and have seen strong gusts of storm in the plains of the south. But to get full expression of the very heart and meaning of wind, there is no place like a Yorkshire moor. I think Scottish breezes are thinner, very bleak and piercing, but not substantial. If you lean on them they will let you fall, but one may rest against a Yorkshire breeze as one would on a quickset hedge. I shall not soon forget – having had the good fortune to meet a vigorous one on an April morning, between Hawes and Settle, just on the flat under Whernside – the vague sense of wonder with which I watched Ingleborough stand without rocking.'

RIBBLEHEAD VIADUCT, BATTY MOSS

Built mainly of Littledale limestone in the 1870s, the Ribblehead Viaduct is 1,328 feet long, has twenty-four arches, and carries the seventy-two-mile Settle-to-Carlisle railway across Batty Moss. The highest arch soars 105 feet above the surrounding moorland. Just north, the Blea Moor tunnel – completed in 1875 – is 2,629 feet long and reaches a maximum depth of some 500 feet. The workers and their families (almost 2,000 people in all) lived in shanty-towns in the vicinity. Those men who constructed the tunnel and its ventilation shafts had only basic tools: they worked by candlelight, and drilled holes by hand for the dynamite to be planted inside the rock. Inside St Leonard's church, Chapel-le-Dale, is a memorial to all of the men, women and children who died during the construction of the railway.

SCALES MOOR, NEAR INGLETON

Although it occupies only a minute fraction of Yorkshire, there is more 'limestone pavement' in the Dales than in any other part of Britain. It was created after Ice Age glaciers had scoured parts of the landscape down to bare limestone rock, exposing a network of thin surface cracks, or joints. Through time, these joints were widened and deepened by the dissolving action of slightly acid rainwater to form fissures, or 'grykes'. The limestone blocks, forming the pavement top, are known as 'clints'. Growing within the grykes (which can vary in width from a few inches to several feet, and can be surprisingly deep) is a large range of plants, including hart's tongue fern and the occasional tree. Underground, the water has created a vast network of potholes, passages and caverns.

DENTDALE, NEAR COWGILL

In his portrait of Dent, entitled *A Memorial by the Trustees of Cowgill Chapel* (1868), Adam Sedgwick, a local man who became Professor of Geology at Cambridge, wrote: 'Trusting in the traditions of family history we may affirm, that after the Reformation, and down towards the concluding part of the last century, Dent was in the enjoyment of happiness and prosperity: in a humble and rustic form, it might be; but with a good base to rest upon – the intelligence and industry of its inhabitants.' In addition to breeding horses, the valley was famous for its exports of butter ('highly salted and packed in firkins'), wool and 'yarn-stockings of the finest quality'. So fast and so furious did everyone knit, that Robert Southey called them the 'Terrible Knitters of Dent'.

SEMER WATER

According to legend, an old man, dressed in rags, trudged wearily up Wensleydale. At Bainbridge, he turned south up the valley of the River Bain and began knocking on doors in the town he found there, asking for something to eat or drink or a bed for the night. All slammed their doors in his face. These included a priest, whose table was laden with fare; and the lord of the castle, who set his dogs on him. Having been spurned by everyone in the town, the old man clambered further up the dale, where he found the humble cottage of a poor shepherd, together with a warm welcome. After blessing his host, the old man cursed the town, bringing down torrents of water from the fells. Next morning, the town had disappeared, and in its place was Semer Water, the largest natural lake in Yorkshire.

THWAITE

Nestling in the valley bottom at the southern foot of Kisdon – the isolated hill that reaches 1,637 feet above sea-level and dominates the head of Swaledale – are the former lead-mining villages of Thwaite and Muker. Their names are derived from Old Norse words: the former meaning 'a woodland clearing', and the latter, 'a small cultivated field'. Thwaite, the smaller of the two villages, is noted for being the birthplace of the Kearton brothers: Richard (1862–1928) and Cherry (1871–1940), pioneers of natural history photography. As sophisticated telephoto lenses and fast film stocks had yet to be developed, the brothers devised other means of getting close to their subjects, including hiding inside a stuffed cow. The stone lintel of their Thwaite home is carved with birds and animals.

UPPER SWALEDALE, NEAR IVELET

Travelling to Richmond through Swaledale in 1771, Arthur Young remarked: 'We looked down from the road on a very beautiful valley of cultivated inclosures on the river, and walled in by high hills. I found the country all moors, and greatly improvable, but – alas! none undertaken.' Later in *A Six Months Tour Through the North of England*, he asked James Croft, a collier-farmer and 'a genius in husbandry', 'if he did not think every part of the moors were highly susceptible of improvement – "Improvement! Sir," he replied with eagerness, "there is not an acre but might be made as good land as a man would wish to farm".' Thereupon, Young tried to secure Croft's release from the coal mine so that he could devote himself to farming and cultivating the moors full-time.

HAY MEADOW, NEAR IVELET

In late June or early July, during an average year, the hay meadows in upper Swaledale, between Gunnerside and Muker, are ablaze with a rich variety of wild flower species, including buttercups, cranesbills and vetches. If, however, these grasslands ceased to be farmed in the traditional way – using natural rather than artificial fertilizers – the diversity of plant species would be greatly diminished as a result. Although artificial fertilizers have been available since the 1950s and can almost double the yield of hay, they do so at the expense of wild flowers. While the hay is growing, sheep and cattle are excluded from the meadows. For convenience, most of the meadows contain a field barn to store the harvested hay.

GUNNERSIDE, UPPER SWALEDALE

In 1761 John Wesley visited Swaledale for the first time. Later, he wrote of country life: 'See that little house, under the wood, by the riverside! There is rural life in perfection. How happy then is the farmer that lives there? Let us take a detail of his happiness. He rises with, or before, the sun . . . He sees to the ploughing and sowing his ground, in winter or in spring. In summer and autumn he hurries and sweats among his mowers and reapers. And where is his happiness in the meantime? . . . Our eyes and ears may convince us there is not a less happy body of men in all England than the country farmers. In general life is supremely dull; and it is usually unhappy too. For of all people in the kingdom they are most discontented; seldom satisfied either with God or man.'

OXNOP SIDE, NEAR SWALEDALE

From its source on the northern heights of Askrigg Common, the Oxnop Beck flows north for a little more than two miles to join the River Swale at Ivelet Bridge. Just before entering Swaledale, the beck tumbles through Oxnop Gill, a wooded ravine, rich in wild life. Since this area was a favourite haunt of the Kearton brothers, pioneers of natural history photography, the wood is now known as Kearton's Wood. Oxnop Hall nearby, with its stone slate roof and mullioned windows, is a fine example of a seventeenth-century Swaledale farmhouse. The wild moorland road running up the valley from Swaledale, passes the crumbling limestone cliffs of Oxnop Scar, climbs over the 1,633-feet-high watershed of Askrigg Common, and then descends into Wensleydale, by way of Askrigg.

SWALEDALE, FROM SATRON MOOR

In *A Tour Thro' the Whole Island of Great Britain*, Daniel Defoe wrote: 'The Swale is a noted river, though not extraordinary large, for giving name to the lands which it runs through for some length, which are called Swale Dale, and to an ancient family of that name, one of whom had the vanity, as I have heard, to boast, that his family was so ancient as not to receive that name from, but to give name to the river itself. One of the worthless successors of this line, who had brought himself to the dignity of

what they call in London, a Fleeter, used to write himself, in his abundant vanity, Sir Solomon Swale, of Swale Hall, in Swale Dale, in the county of Swale in the North Riding of York.' (A 'fleeter' is a shifty person or a fugitive – in this case, probably from creditors.)

OLD GANG MINES, SWALEDALE

Although lead ore has been extracted from the Yorkshire Dales since prehistoric times, it was not until the seventeenth century that mining on an intensive scale began.

In the triangle of land between Swaledale and Arkengarthdale the landscape is littered with the decaying remains of spoil heaps, smelting hearths, peat stores and chimneys. The ruins of the Old Gang mining complex stand in the valley of Hard Level Gill, a mile or so upstream from Surrender Bridge (on the road between Feetham in Swaledale and Arkengarthdale). At the beginning of the nineteenth century, Britain was the world's largest exporter of lead; by the end of the century, mining in the Dales had virtually ceased, due to cheaper imports from abroad.

ARKENGARTHDALE

In a letter to American poet and essayist Ralph Waldo Emerson, dated 8 May 1841, the Scottish historian Thomas Carlyle wrote: 'For ten days, I rode or sauntered among Yorkshire fields and knolls; the sight of the young Spring, new to me these seven years, was beautiful, or better than beauty. Solitude itself, the great Silence of the Earth, was as balm to this weary, sick heart of mine; not Dragons of Wantley (so they call Lord Wharncliffe, the wooden Tory man), not babbling itinerant Barrister people, fox-hunting Aristocracy, not Yeomanry Captains cultivating milk-white mustachios, nor the perpetual racket, and "dinner at eight o'clock," could altogether countervail the fact that green Earth was around one and unadulterated sky overhead, and the voice of waters and birds, – not the foolish speech of Cockneys at all times!'

ARKENGARTHDALE

A tributary valley of Swaledale, Arkengarthdale is the most northerly valley in the Yorkshire Dales National Park. Rising on moorland to the east of Tan Hill, the Arkle Beck flows south-eastward down the dale – past the settlements of Whaw, Eskeleth, Langthwaite, Arkle Town and Booze – to the market town of Reeth, above the River Swale. 'Arkengarthdale' is of Norse origin and means 'the valley of Arkil's garth' or field. During Norman times it was the hunting preserve of the lords of Richmond. Today, the fellsides bear the scars of lead-mining, an industry that flourished in the dale until the end of the nineteenth century. Coal to fuel the smelting furnaces around Langthwaite was transported by road from Tan Hill colliery.

FIELD BARN, NEAR KELD

Most of the drystone walls of the Dales landscape were constructed between 1760 and 1820, when Parliament passed a series of Enclosure Acts, enabling landowners to create neat rectangular fields of 8 to 12 acres out of what was previously unfenced common land. In most of these fields, a two-storeyed, stone barn was built to store hay and house cattle over the winter months. Names for these barns vary depending on the area: in Swaledale they are known as 'field-houses' or 'cow-houses'; while in Wharfedale and Craven they are called 'laithes'. They also vary in size and style; those in the south tending to be larger. The combination of stone walls and fields barns is a distinctive feature of the landscape of the Yorkshire Dales, and is found nowhere else in Britain.

PRY HILL, NEAR KELD

The remote, former lead-mining village of Keld, 1,100 feet above sea-level, stands on a steep headland, overlooking the swift-flowing River Swale and the enclosed pastures of Pry Hill (the southern spur of Black Moor, to the north). The name 'Keld' is an old Norse word meaning 'a place by a river'. In the vicinity of Keld, the Swale has cut through the layers of limestone to produce an impressive collection of waterfalls. Kisdon Force, less than a mile downstream from Keld, is considered to be the most dramatic. The Pennine Way, the long-distance footpath, passes within a few hundred yards of the village – with its sandstone houses, Post Office, chapel and Youth Hostel (formerly a shooting lodge) – and many walkers make the detour for rest and refreshment.

HIGH FRITH, WEST STONES DALE

Although much of the undulating moorland, north of upper Swaledale is wild and desolate, parts of it have been enclosed by drystone walls, notably along the valley of the Stonedale Beck (or West Stones Dale). Many of the enclosures contain field barns. Keld, the village nearest the scattered farmsteads of West Stones Dale, was once home to Neddy Dick, hailed by some as an unschooled musical genius. After discovering that certain pieces of limestone, when struck by another, created a musical note, he collected enough rocks to produce a complete scale. But his ambition to tour England in a donkey cart with his 'rock band' never materialized. Some time after his death in 1928, the rocks were destroyed when the outhouse in which they were stored was demolished.

EAST STONESDALE, NEAR KELD

The desolate moorland around East and West Stonesdale is pitted with the derelict remains of coal-mining. During the eighteenth and nineteenth centuries, before the Settle to Carlisle railway line brought cheaper and better coal from Durham and South Yorkshire, the fuel was used for lead-smelting, lime-burning and domestic fires. The remote Tan Hill Inn, on Stonesdale Moor, probably owes its existence to the collieries that have been worked in the locality since at least the thirteenth century. Not only did it provide hospitality for the miners and their families, the inn was also used, among others, by Scottish drovers on their journey south. At 1,732 feet above sea-level, it holds the record for being the highest public house in Britain.

LUNEDALE, NEAR GRASSHOLME

Rising on the hostile, uninhabited wilderness of the High Pennines – east of Appleby-in-Westmorland – the River Lune (not the Lancashire Lune) flows eastward to join the Tees, near Middleton-in-Teesdale. In length, from source to Tees, it is less than twelve miles. Although the construction of the Grassholme Reservoir, in the lower part of Lunedale, began in 1910, work was not finally completed until 1924. The Selset Reservoir, situated higher up the dale, was built in 1961. From Grassholme, the Pennine Way heads northward – through lush pastures, enclosed by drystone walls – to pass the prominent landmark of Kirkcarrion, a walled plantation of trees on the summit of a round hill. Being the site of a tumulus, or ancient burial mound, it is reputed to be haunted.

BALDERSDALE, FROM HURY RESERVOIR

In 1973, the High Pennine daleswoman, Hannah Hauxwell, was first introduced to the general public in the Yorkshire Television documentary *Too Long A Winter*. At the time, despite her white hair, she was only forty-six. Living alone in the remote Baldersdale farm of Low Birk Hatt – with no electricity and no water on tap – her story touched the hearts of millions. Suddenly she found herself a celebrity. On those occasions when there was not enough water in the stream or rainwater tub, she did her washing in the nearby reservoir. In 1988 failing strength forced her to leave Low Birk Hatt, where she had lived since she was three. Yet, even with all mod cons, central heating, hot running water and a flush toilet, in her new home, it was in Baldersdale that her heart belonged.

EGGLESTONE ABBEY

Occupying a hill – on the old Yorkshire side of the River Tees, just over a mile south-east of Barnard Castle – the abbey of St Mary & St John the Baptist at Egglestone was founded at the end of the twelfth century by Ralph de Multon, and colonized by Premonstratensian canons from Easby Abbey. Through-out its history, the abbey was not large, or important, or wealthy.

Indeed, it suffered so severely from financial difficulties that at one stage it was almost reduced to the status of a priory. It also suffered at the hands of marauding English and Scottish armies. After its dissolution in 1540, part of the abbey was converted into a manorial hall. Over subsequent centuries most of the buildings were demolished and their stone used in other buildings. The ruins that remain of the abbey are now in the care of English Heritage.

RICHMOND CASTLE

Daniel Defoe, in *A Tour Thro' the Whole Island of Great Britain*, wrote in about 1725: 'This town of Richmond . . . is walled, and had a strong castle; but as those things are now all slighted, so really the account of them is of small consequence, and needless; old fortifications being, if fortification was wanted, of very little signification; the River Swale runs under the wall of this castle, and has some unevenness at its bottom, by reason of rocks which intercept its passage, so that it falls like a cataract, but not with so great a noise.' Situated at the entrance to Swaledale, the old woollen market town grew up around the Norman castle, which was founded by Alan the Red in 1071. The name 'Richmond' is derived from the French *Riche-mont*, meaning 'strong hill'.

EASBY ABBEY, NEAR RICHMOND

Joseph Mallord William Turner visited Easby Abbey – which is found on the north bank of the River Swale, less than a mile south-east of Richmond – during his tour through the north of England in 1797. On that day, Monday, 29 July, he travelled some twenty-five miles, starting at Aysgarth and finishing at Richmond. He also made forty sketches, which not only included studies of Easby Abbey, but views of Bolton Castle, Marrick Priory, Swaledale and Richmond. He revisited Easby Abbey in 1816, and in the finished water-colour (c.1818) he included a mallard (the wild duck being a pun on the 'Mallord' part of his name). Founded in about 1155 for Premonstratensian canons and dedicated to St Agatha, the abbey was demolished after the Dissolution in the sixteenth century. The ruins are now in the care of English Heritage.

MIDDLEHAM CASTLE, WENSLEYDALE

The earthwork remains of the first castle at Middleham, built to guard the entrances to Coverdale and Wensleydale, date from about 1086 when Alan, Earl of Richmond, granted the manor to his younger brother, Ribald. The present castle, which stands some 500 yards north-east of the earlier stronghold, is thought to date from the mid-twelfth century when the massive, rectangular keep (one of the largest in England) was erected. In the thirteenth century the stronghold became the property of the Neville family, but it was forfeited to the Crown in 1471, when Richard, Earl of Warwick, the 'Kingmaker', was killed at the battle of Barnet. After eventually falling into disrepair, some of the stone was removed from the site and used as building material. The ruins are now in the care of English Heritage.

JERVAULX ABBEY

The Cistercian monastery at Jervaulx, on the banks of the River Ure between Middleham and Masham, was originally founded in 1145 at Fors, near Askrigg, for Savignac monks from Byland Abbey. The community moved to Jervaulx in 1156, nine years after the Savignac and Cistercian Orders were united. In addition to sheep farming and mining for lead, iron and coal, the abbey's monks became famous for breeding horses and were, reputedly, responsible for making the first Wensleydale cheese. The abbey was destroyed by Henry VIII in 1537 and the last abbot – together with more than 200 others, including Robert Aske, the leader of the Yorkshire insurrection – executed for his involvement in the revolt known as The Pilgrimage of Grace. The name 'Jervaulx' is derived from Yoredale (the vale of the Yore or Ure).

DRUID'S TEMPLE, NEAR ILTON

Despite its appearance, the Druid's Temple – hidden in a conifer plantation some four miles south-west of Masham – is not of ancient origin. In fact, it is a folly, erected in about 1820 by William Danby of nearby Swinton Hall, and based on an original plan by P. T. Runton. Although it was inspired by Stonehenge, the 'temple' is built in the shape of a lozenge more than a hundred feet long and fifty feet wide. Each of the stone arrangements has been given a name: The Two Outer Guards; The Two Inner Guards; The Sacrificial Altar; The Four Columns; The Phallus; The Wardens or Priests; The Master or Hierophant; The Two Guards of the Solar Temple; The Solar Temple; and The Tomb. The massive stone lintel over the entrance is more than ten feet long. Amid the surrounding trees are various mock 'standing stones'.

BRIMHAM ROCKS, BRIMHAM MOOR

On Brimham Moor overlooking Nidderdale – three miles east of Pateley Bridge and almost 1,000 feet above sea-level – are a strange and fantastic collection of massive gritstone rock formations, created by the erosive action of the elements over a period of thousands of years. Many of the naturally sculpted shapes resemble objects – animate and inanimate – and have, therefore, acquired names such as the Dancing Bear, the Cannon and the Yoke of Oxen. The Idol Rock, weighing an estimated 180 tons, is perched precariously on a tiny pedestal about one and a half feet at its narrowest. In the late eighteenth and early nineteenth centuries their origin was attributed to the Druids. Brimham Rocks and Brimham House, built as a shooting lodge in 1792, now belong to the National Trust.

ABBOT HUBY'S TOWER, FOUNTAINS ABBEY

Sheltered in the wooded valley of the River Skell, three miles south-west of Ripon, are the impressive remains of Fountains Abbey, once one of the richest religious houses in England. Founded in 1132 by dissident Benedictine monks from St Mary's Abbey at York, the monastery was admitted to the Cistercian Order in 1135. Although the abbey's main source of wealth was wool, income also came from mining, quarrying, farming and horse breeding. The monastery was surrendered to the Crown in 1539. In the photograph are the remains of the east end of the church, including the 160-feet-high tower built by Abbot Marmaduke Huby in about 1500. On the left, obscuring the south transept, is the shell of the chapter house. The ruins now form part of the Studley Royal Estate, owned by the National Trust.

NAVE AISLE, FOUNTAINS ABBEY

Turner visited Fountains Abbey during his North-of-England tour of 1797 and sketched several views, including the east end of the church and Abbot Huby's tower. In the following year he exhibited at the Royal Academy a watercolour painting entitled *The Dormitory and Transept of Fountain's Abbey – Evening.* The following lines from *The Seasons* by James Thomson (1700–1748) accompanied the painting:

All ether soft'ning sober evening takes
Her wonted station in the middle air;
A thousand shadows at her beck –
In circle following circle, gathers round
To close the face of things.

It has been said of Turner that his interest in painting the view was more piscatorial than picturesque; for, being a keen fisherman, he included one figure fishing and another sketching.

TEMPLE OF PIETY, STUDLEY ROYAL

In 1699, when John Aislabie inherited the Studley Estate, the adjoining remains of Fountains Abbey belonged to the Messenger family. His plans to landscape the grounds did not initially include the ruins, but it soon became apparent that their addition would provide a spectacular completion to the overall scheme. The Messengers, however, would not sell. Eventually, in 1768, Aislabie's son, William, persuaded the Messenger family to change its mind. By that stage, the picturesque romantic style was becoming fashionable, and William's addition of the ruins to his grounds emphasized the wild and dramatic features of the lower Skell valley, in direct contrast to the ordered formality of his father's water garden. The Temple of Piety was so-named by William as a memorial to his father.

DEVIL'S ARROWS, NEAR BOROUGHBRIDGE

Standing in a field west of Borough-bridge – once an important coaching stop on the Great North road – are three gritstone pillars, each protruding about twenty feet above ground. Dating from the Bronze Age, these monoliths are thought to have been transported from a quarry near Knaresborough, seven miles south-west. According to legend, the Devil took a strong dislike to the nearby settlement at Aldborough and determined to destroy it. For some reason, however, he warned the inhabitants of Boroughbridge of his intention: 'Borobrigg keep out of the way. For Audboro' town I will ding down.' He then climbed to the top of How Hill (south-west of Ripon) and threw four huge stones towards Aldborough, each missile falling short of its intended target. The fourth stone has long since disappeared.

ST MARY'S CHURCH, THIRSK

Dating from the fifteenth century, St Mary's Church at Thirsk is considered the best example of Perpendicular architecture to be found in Yorkshire. Its battlemented west tower, the first part of the church to be built, is eighty feet high. Situated in the fertile Vale of Mowbray, the market town is divided by the Cod Beck into two parts: to the east is Old Thirsk, centred around its village green, formerly the market place; while to the west is New Thirsk, established in the eighteenth century when the town became an important staging point on the coaching route between London and the north-east. James Herriot, the famous author and vet, based the fictional 'Darrowby' on the town, where in real life (as Alf Wight) he worked. He married Helen (really Joan Danbury) in Thirsk Church.

SOUTH WOODS, SUTTON BANK

From Sutton Bank, where the North York Moors National Park has an information centre, there are walks and nature trails along the top of the escarpment and down the steep wooded slopes to Lake Gormire. Legend says that the lake – formed during the Ice Age when a landslide blocked part of a glacial meltwater channel – is haunted by a white horse and its rider who fell to their deaths from the top of White-stone Cliff (or White Mare Crag) above. William and Dorothy Wordsworth visited the spot in 1802. Dorothy wrote in her diary: 'As we descended the hill there was no distinct view, but of a great space; only near us we saw the wild (and as people say) bottomless tarn in the hollow at the side of the hill. It seemed to be made visible to us only by its own light, for the hill above us was dark.'

CLEVELAND HILLS ESCARPMENT

This photograph of the steep north-western escarpment of the North York Moors was taken from Park Dyke, looking south-west across the wooded slopes of Battersby Moor and the cultivated valley of Ingleby Botton to the distant hills of Urra Moor and Cold Moor. At 1,489 feet above sea-level, Round Hill on Urra Moor is the highest point in the National Park. Near the Bronze Age burial mound and Ordnance Survey triangulation pillar that mark the summit is an eighteenth-century handstone indicating the direction to 'Stoxla' (Stokesley) and 'Kirby' (Kirbymoorside). A short distance further east is an older stone – a boundary marker situated at the junction of several moorland tracks. As it has a face carved on one side, it is known as the Face Stone.

HAMBLETON HILLS, FROM SUTTON BANK

Forming the western boundary of the North York Moors, the steep, wooded escarpment of the Hambleton Hills sweep northward from near Sutton Bank to meet the Cleveland Hills beyond Thimbleby Moor. The Hambleton Road, a rough moorland track running along the crest of the hills, is part of an ancient highway (in use since prehistoric times) linking Scotland with the south of England. The use of the track by drovers (mainly those taking cattle from Scotland to markets at York and Malton) reached its peak in the eighteenth and nineteenth centuries, after the introduction of turnpike roads, which proved costly and time-consuming. Droving declined with the arrival of the railways, and by the beginning of the twentieth century moving cattle long distances on foot had ceased.

PARISH CHURCH, GREAT AYTON

Captain James Cook may have been born at Marton (now a suburb of Middlesbrough) on 27 October 1728, but the village most popularly associated with him is Great Ayton. From 1736, when the family moved to Aireyholme Farm, Cook went to the village school (rebuilt in 1785 and now the Captain Cook Museum), and attended services in the parish church of All Saints. His mother, Grace, lies buried in the churchyard; as does Thomas Skottowe, Cook's benefactor and his father's employer. The cottage in Easby Lane, reputedly occupied by Cook's parents in retirement, was dismantled in 1934 and re-erected in Melbourne, Victoria, Australia. Its original site is now marked by an obelisk from Cape Everard, near Point Hicks – the first place in Australia to be sighted from Cook's *Endeavour* on 20 April 1770.

CLEVELAND PLAIN, FROM THE WAINSTONES

Above the dark conifers of Broughton Bank – on the north-facing escarpment of the Cleveland Hills and overlooking the arable fields of the Cleveland Plain – are a series of rock outcrops known as the Wainstones. These heavily-eroded sandstone crags, or 'edges', are popular with rock climbers, and are situated on both the Cleveland Way and the Lyke Wake Walk. (The village in the middle of the photograph is Great Broughton; to the left is Kirkby; with Stokesley beyond. On the horizon, some ten miles away, is Middlesbrough and industrial Teesside). In *A Six Months Tour Through the North of England* (1771), Arthur Young wrote of the 'immense plain, comprehending almost all Cleveland finely cultivated, the verdure beautiful and the enclosures, adding prodigiously to the view.'

ST ANDREWS CHURCH, INGLEBY GREENHOW

At the north-western extremity of the National Park, the small village of Ingleby Greenhow lies on the edge of the Cleveland Plain at the foot of the steep escarpment of the Cleveland Hills, three miles south-east of Great Ayton. The Norman parish church of St Andrew, with its squat little bell-turret, was almost entirely rebuilt in 1741. It was granted to Whitby Abbey in a charter drawn up between 1143 and 1147 by Adam, son of Viel (or Vitalis), of Ingleby Manor 'for the salvation of my soul'. During the nineteenth century, wagons of iron ore from the Rosedale mines, situated some fourteen miles away, were lowered by steel cables from the top of the escarpment at Greenhow down the steep, 1,430-yard-long (1-in-5 gradient) Ingleby Incline to Battersby (originally Ingleby) Junction.

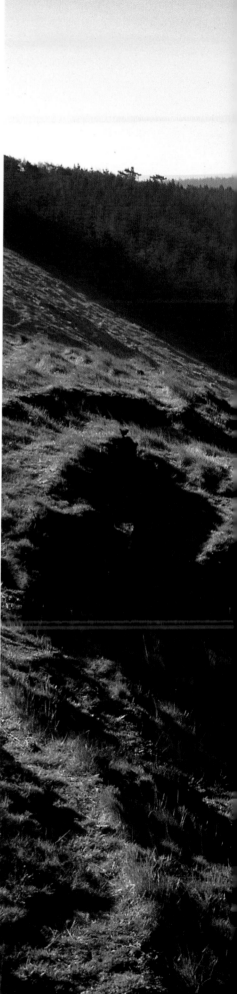

ROSEBERRY TOPPING

Rising 1,051 feet above sea-level, the distinctive hooked pinnacle of Roseberry Topping stands at the north-western corner of the North York Moors, overlooking 'Captain Cook Country' and the Cleveland Plain. Danish settlers, regarding the isolated hill as sacred, called it 'Othensbergh', or the 'hill of Odin'. In 1586, William Camden referred to it as 'Ounesbery Topping' and wrote: 'It is the landmark that directs sailors, and a prognostic to the neighbours hereabouts. For when its top begins to be darkened with clouds, rain generally follows.' 'Roseberry' may derive from 'rhos', a 'moor', and 'berg', a 'hill'. Originally conical, the hill's shape has been considerably altered due to extensive quarrying and mining activity carried out in the nineteenth century.

CAPTAIN COOK'S MONUMENT, FROM GREAT AYTON MOOR

'Captain Cook Country' stretches from the Yorkshire coast at Whitby to the River Tees, and includes a large swathe of the North York Moors National Park. The monument on the 1,064-feet-high summit of Easby Moor, near Great Ayton, was erected in 1827 by Robert Campion, a Whitby banker. It was at the ancient fishing port of Whitby that James Cook, the son of a farm labourer, learned his trade as a merchant seaman. He joined the Royal Navy in 1755 and spent much of the next twelve years charting the coasts of Canada and Newfoundland. In 1768 he was given command of the Whitby-built *Endeavour* in which, with Joseph Banks and other scientists, he sailed to Tahiti, New Zealand and Australia. In 1779, on his third voyage of discovery, he was killed by natives at Kealakekua Bay, Hawaii.

BOULBY CLIFF, FROM STAITHES

Officially opened in May 1969, the 108-mile-long Cleveland Way – starting in the market town of Helmsley and finishing at the coastal resort of Filey – traverses Boulby Cliff, near Staithes, scarred with centuries of quarrying and mining. At 666 feet above sea-level, the cliff is the highest point on England's east coast. Once worked for alum (a chemical used in the tanning and dyeing industries), Boulby became the site of Britain's first potash mine and refinery when building commenced in 1969. Its main shaft is more than 3,750 feet deep, with workings extending some two miles under the seabed. Since 1981 the mine, situated within the North Moors National Park, has also produced salt – most of which is used by local authorities for de-icing roads in winter.

BOULBY CLIFF

A graphic record of alum mining at Boulby appears in *The History of Cleveland* (1808) by the Rev. John Graves: 'These works are situated on the verge of a stupendous cliff; and the rock, cut down by an almost Herculean labour, discovers the different strata in the bowels of the earth, and affords a spectacle at once pleasing, awful, and magnificent. As the alum rock lies at a considerable depth the labour of removing it is attended with much labour and expense; but this part of the business is conducted with such order and regularity, as not only to equalise the labour to the strength of the different workmen, but also to enforce it in proportion to their wages. For this purpose, they have wheel-barrows of various sizes . . . for which wages are paid in proportion.'

STAITHES

None of the tightly packed houses that spill down the steep cliffside at Staithes has a number: all are identified by names. Traditionally, the fishermen called their homes after the names of their cobles – for example, 'Refuge Cottage', 't Star of Hope Cottage' and 'Waverley'. 'Captain Cook's Cottage', however, is named after the celebrated explorer, who – prior to leaving for Whitby in 1746 – was apprenticed to the grocer and haberdasher William Sanderson. The shop, which overlooked the harbour, has long disappeared, washed away by the sea. It is said that some of its material was salvaged to build the cottage now named after the captain. Oddly, with a few exceptions, the roofs of those houses that face the sea at Staithes have red pantiles; those facing away, grey slate.

COBLES, PORT MULGRAVE

Under the headline 'Brussels sinks humble coble' the *Observer* (11 February 1996) reported that the forced reduction of the English fishing fleet by European regulations meant the demise of the traditional, flat-bottomed fishing boat of the north-east. Said to have been modelled on the Viking longship, the ancient coble – with its deep bow and shallow stern – was designed to be launched and landed bow first on open beaches, even in raging surf. By being 'clinker-built' – constructed of overlapping 'strakes,' or planks – the boat achieved maximum strength with minimum weight. According to Steve Cook of Whitby – 'the last coble builder on the north-east coast of England' – 'I used to be paid to build them, but now I get paid to destroy them. It's madness.'

LINGROW KNOCK & KETTLE NESS, FROM PORT MULGRAVE

'The approach of sunset was so very beautiful, so grand in its masses of splendidly-coloured clouds, that there was quite an assemblage on the walk along the cliff . . . to enjoy the beauty. Before the sun dipped below the black mass of Kettleness, standing boldly athwart the western sky, its downward way was marked by myriad clouds of every sunset-colour – flame, purple, pink, green, violet, and all the tints of gold; with here and there masses not large, but of seemingly absolute blackness, in all sorts of shapes, as well outlined as colossal silhouettes. The experience was not lost on the painters, and doubtless some of the sketches of the *Prelude to the Great Storm* will grace R. A. and R. I. walls in May next.' (*Dracula*: Bram Stoker)

RUNSWICK BAY

Because the cliffs supporting the fishing village of Runswick Bay are unstable, the settlement has suffered repeatedly from landslips. One night in 1682, specifically, every house in the village, except one, fell into the sea. The story is that many of the inhabitants were attending a wake at the time. After realizing that the ground was moving, they quickly alerted the rest of the community, all of whom fled to safety. In the morning the only house left standing was that in which the wake was held. The village was subsequently rebuilt. In order to try to prevent further slippages, a sea wall was constructed in 1970. The thatched house in the photograph, nearest the shore, was once a coastguard's cottage. It is now a grace-and-favour residence of the Marquis of Normanby.

RUNSWICK BAY

Legend says that one of the sea caves, in the cliffs south of the village of Runswick Bay, was inhabited by a hob, who could cure whooping cough. Mothers took their sickly children to the cave – known as Hob's Hole – and invoked the goblin's help by chanting: 'Hob-hole Hob! My bairn's gotten t'kink cough, Tak't off! Tak't off!' Most local super-stitions, however, were associated with the fishing industry. If a fisherman, for example, saw a woman while walking down to his boat in the morning, he would abandon fishing for that day. During a storm, children would dance around a fire on the clifftop and sing: 'Souther wind, souther, and blow father home to mother.' When the fleet returned safely after a severe storm, the fishermen's wives would give thanks by sacrificing a cat.

KETTLE NESS & RUNSWICK BAY

Like many other parts of the Yorkshire coast, the cliffs of Kettle Ness, east of Runswick Bay, have suffered dramatically from coastal erosion. On the night of 17 December 1829 much of the clifftop hamlet of Kettleness, including the alum works, slid into the sea. The tragic loss of many coastal villages and houses – especially in Holderness, dubbed 'the fastest eroding coastline in Europe' – seems to have rapidly escalated in recent years. In 1996, near Hornsea, a farmer watched helplessly as her clifftop home – condemned as dangerous – was demolished for her own safety. On average, erosion along the Holderness coastline occurs at the rate of as much as ten feet a year. Yorkshire is not only becoming smaller, it is also moving further away from the Continent.

SANDSEND, NEAR WHITBY

In September 1994, the sinking of the yacht *Akiba* – intercepted at sea by HM Customs officers and lost off Whitby while under tow – sparked a frenzy of activity along the seventeen-mile stretch of coast between Sandsend and Saltburn-by-the-Sea. Although Customs knew where the vessel went down, it had been swept away by powerful underwater currents. In consequence, all manner of people who seldom, if ever, visited the beach suddenly found an excuse to be there. Aware or not that their every move was under constant surveillance, they were perhaps hoping to come across part of the vessel's valuable and illegal cargo – two tons of Moroccan black cannabis resin, broken down and sealed in manageable watertight packages, and rumoured to be worth £5 million.

ST OSWALD'S CHURCH, LYTHE

The parish church at Lythe was essentially rebuilt in 1910 with stone quarried from the nearby cliffs of Sandsend Ness. During the church's construction, a number of carved cross-heads and hog-back gravestones were discovered, dating back to the ninth and tenth centuries. Inside the church there are several memorials to the Phipps family of nearby Mulgrave Castle (now owned by the Marquis of Normanby). Old Mulgrave Castle (the remains of which stand in Mulgrave Woods) is said to have been built by the legendary giant Wade, who lived there with his equally enormous wife, Bell. According to one story, Bell built Pickering Castle at the same time. But, since they had only one hammer between them, it was thrown back and forth across the Moors each time one or the other needed to use it.

SANDSEND NESS

The cliffs of Sandsend Ness, north-west of Whitby, consist mainly of layers of sedimentary rocks, including the shales from which alum was extracted. At the top of the cliffs is the Dogger sandstone, capped by a layer of boulder clay. At the bottom are layers of jet rock (formed from the fossilized driftwood of ancient monkey-puzzle-type trees), and containing the hard, black Whitby jet that can be carved and polished to make jewellery and ornaments. Sandwiched between the two is a complex series of shales.

Although North Yorkshire's alum industry started near Guisborough in about 1600, quarrying of the cliffs at Sandsend did not start until the eighteenth century. Among the chemicals used to produce alum was ammonia in the form of human urine.

CRETEBLOCK, WHITBY SCAUR

During the First World War, a shortage of steel led to the construction of a number of 'experimental' ships out of ferro-concrete (reinforced concrete). One of the first of these vessels to be built in Britain was a lighter, launched from the docks at Whitby in 1919. The enduring remains of another, the tug *Creteblock*, stand on Whitby Scaur. However, unlike the majority of vessels wrecked off the Yorkshire coast, the *Creteblock* – the first part of its name derived from 'concrete' – was sunk intentionally after the Second World War. In 1934, seven years after losing its Lloyd's classification, the boat was dismantled and its hulk laid up in the upper harbour. On 22 August 1948, the obstruction was towed out to sea, but instead of ending up in deep water it was sunk on the Scaur.

OLD TOWN, WHITBY

Bram Stoker visited the old whaling port of Whitby in 1890. 'This is a lovely place,' he wrote in a letter. 'The little river, the Esk, runs through a deep valley which broadens out as it comes near the harbour. A great viaduct runs across, through which the view seems somehow further away than it really is. The houses of the old town – the side away from us – are all red-roofed and seem piled one over the other anyhow. Right over the town is the ruin of Whitby Abbey . . . It is a most noble ruin, of immense size,

and full of beautiful and romantic bits; there is a legend that a white lady is seen in one of the windows. Between it and the town there is another church, the parish one, round which is a big graveyard, all full of tombstones. This is, to my mind, the nicest spot in Whitby.'

BLACK NAB, SALTWICK BAY

On the evening tide of 9 May 1997 a replica of Captain Cook's *Endeavour* sailed past the dark brooding headlands of Black Nab and Saltwick Nab, and into the historic

harbour at Whitby, where it was welcomed with a gun salute and a flotilla of decorated boats. The ship, built in Freemantle, Western Australia, had set sail for England some seven months earlier, on 16 October 1996. It was from Whitby, in 1768, that Captain James Cook sailed in the original HM Bark *Endeavour* to search for a mythical Great Southern Continent. Before being purchased by the Royal Navy, the squat, sturdy, flat-bottomed vessel was known as *The Earl of Pembroke*. It was built in Whitby in 1765 as a three-masted collier, or 'cat'.

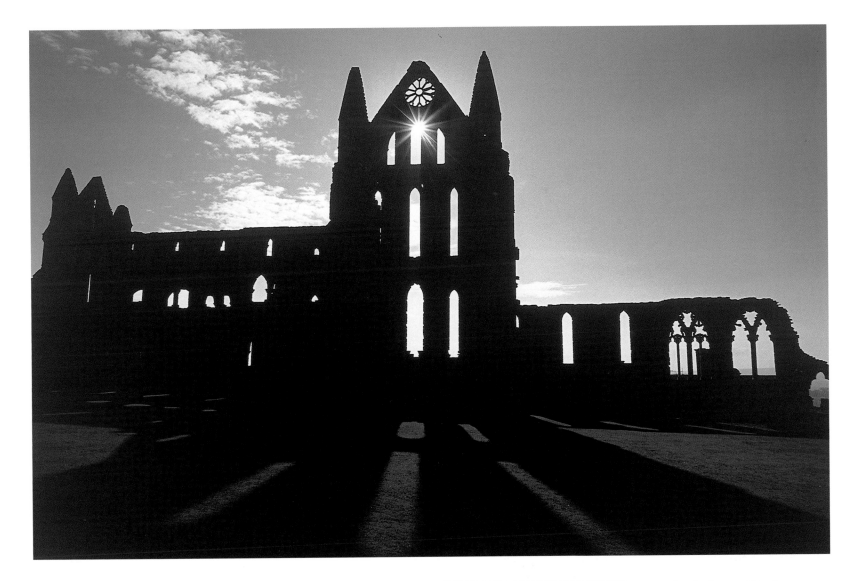

SALTWICK BAY

Early in the morning of 30 October 1914, the *Rohilla*, a Red Cross hospital ship belonging to the British India Steam Navigation Company, foundered on a reef just north of Saltwick Bay, with the tragic loss of many lives. At 7,409 tons, it was one of the largest vessels to be wrecked off the Yorkshire coast. Of the 229 crew, medical staff and nurses on board the ill-fated ship, 145 of them managed to survive due to the heroic courage of the lifeboat crews, who time after time braved mountainous seas to effect their rescue. One lifeboat, in fact, had to be manhandled overland to the top of Saltwick Nab, from where it was lowered down the precipitous cliffs to the sea. Having left Queensferry, Firth of Forth, the previous day, the ship was bound for Dunkirk and the evacuation of wounded First World War soldiers from France.

WHITBY ABBEY

Crowning the prominent heights of the East Cliff, where the Romans may have erected a signal station, is the distinctive landmark of Whitby Abbey – or, as it more accurately should be described, the roofless shell of its church. First founded for both men and women by St Hilda in AD 657, the monastery at 'Streaneshalch' (Whitby) soon became a great centre of learning. It was also the home of Brother Caedmon, who died in 680 and whose monument, in the form of a twenty-feet-high cross, stands at the top of the 199 steps leading up to the abbey from the Old Town. According to Bede, none could compare to Caedmon as a poet 'for he did not learn the art of poetry from men, but from God.' Destroyed by the Danes in 867, the monastery was refounded as a Benedictine priory in about 1077. By 1109 it had become an abbey.

LEALHOLM MOOR

In 1847, on his way to become the 'Vicar of Danby' (the living of which he held for nearly fifty-three years), the Reverend Atkinson found himself on Lealholm Moor, alone and uncertain as to the direction he should take: 'Before me, looking westward, was moor, with a valley on the left, and on the right, to the north, an expanse of cultivated land beyond. Across the valley . . . there was moor again; and the valley was, it was clear, but a narrow one; while behind me, as I knew lay three good miles of moor, and nothing but moor. It was a solitude, and a singularly lonely solitude. The only signs of life were given by the grouse, or the half-wild sheep, whose fleeces here and there flecked the brown moor with white spots. It was a wild as well as lonely solitude; and yet not dreary . . .'

QUAKERS' TROD, NEAR COMMONDALE

Although many of the tracks across the moors may have prehistoric origins, the stone-flagged causeways, or 'trods', date from the medieval period. Laid down across boggy moorland to provide a firm, dry passage for heavily laden packhorses, they were essential to the

whole economy of the region. The main trade was wool and by the end of the thirteenth century some 70,000 fleeces were produced annually on the moors, to be shipped to European markets from Whitby and York. Some of the causeways were established as monastic routes, linking abbeys to outlying granges, while others – if their names are to be believed – were attributed to smugglers, Quakers and panniermen. Many routes lead to bridges, such as Beggar's Bridge at Glaisdale and Duck Bridge at Danby.

COMMONDALE MOOR, FROM WAYWORTH MOOR

The rocks of the North York Moors belong entirely to the Jurassic period and were formed by sediment laid down horizontally on the bed of a tropical sea more than 140 million years ago. Comprised of layers of shales, sandstones and limestones, this sea bed was subsequently forced upwards and tilted towards the south by cataclysmic movements in the earth's crust. Later on, the hills and dales were shaped and moulded by the erosive effect of wind and rain, together with numerous and sometimes dramatic changes in the climate. During the various Ice Ages, glacial action smoothed the surface of the hills, deepened the dales and deposited the clay, boulders and stones that can be seen by the visitor today. However, it was the activities of man, rather than any natural forces, that transformed much of what was once a forest into the present moorland landscape.

CASTLETON RIGG & WESTERDALE, FROM WESTERDALE MOOR

'I once heard a very taking and comprehensively descriptive remark,' wrote the Rev. Atkinson, 'made by a man who had seen much in foreign travel as well as in home rambles, in regard to the diversified sections and aspects of these dales of ours and their characteristic scenery. He said: "They differ from all other I have ever seen, and in this particular especially, that elsewhere you have to go in search of beautiful views; here they come and offer themselves to be looked at." That is true; and necessary true when the contours and configurations of the district are borne in mind. For the advance or retrogression of a hundred yards or so will remove the obstacle to vision . . . and permit one to gaze at will on some varied or romantic scene alike unexpected and unforeseen.'

WESTERN HOWES & WESTERDALE MOOR, FROM CASTLETON RIGG

In *A Six Months Tour of the North of England* (1771), Arthur Young, an English writer and agriculturist wrote: '. . . the greatest curiosity to be met with in this country is the vast moors, which are 3, 4, and 5 miles over . . . They consist of a soft, spongy, loose soil, as if composed of rotten vegetables. It is all what they call turf, and is dug into square pieces for burning; when dried it is light as a feather, and burns excellently. Over all the moors it lays in an even stratum, about five or six feet deep, upon a bed of stiff blue and black clay. In digging it away they frequently find vast fir trees, perfectly sound, and some oaks, but not so good as the firs. The body of a man was also found, the flesh was black, but perfectly preserved; after a short exposure to the air, it crumbled into powder.'

DANBY DALE

'Yes, I have seen some winter weather in this out-of-the-way place,' wrote the Vicar of Danby, the Rev. J. C. Atkinson in *Forty Years in a Moorland Parish*, first published in 1891. 'I have seen the snow gathered in drifts of fifteen, eighteen, twenty feet in thickness; I have seen it gathering, piling itself up in fantastic wreaths, sometimes busy only in accumulating substance and solidity, like a yeoman of the elder days, and gathering at the rate of six feet or seven feet in thickness in from twelve hours to twenty-four. And once I saw it gathering – and gathering a foot deep in the hour, moreover – before ever a flake of new snow had fallen, and when the old snow was caked over with a crisp crust, the result of diurnal or sun-thaws and nocturnal freezings again.'

DANBY HEAD, FROM HIGH CRAG

Winter in the North York Moors is often harsh, with heavy falls of snow creating enormous hardship for the farmers, whose sheep are often left out on the high heather moorlands to forage for themselves. The farm in the photograph, 'St Helena', lies at the head of Danby Dale. At its mouth, or 'end' – in the heart of Esk Dale – lies the small village of Danby and the Danby Lodge Moors Centre, which contains a wealth of information about the National Park. The parish church, dedicated to St Hilda, stands in lonely isolation on the eastern side of Danby Dale, some two miles south-west of the village. Buried in the churchyard is the Rev. John Christopher Atkinson (1814–1900), the Danby vicar and historian who wrote the minor classic *Forty Years in a Moorland Parish*.

LITTLE FRYUP DALE, FROM DALE HEAD

During the latter half of the nineteenth century, when the Rev. Atkinson was Vicar of Danby, the belief in fairies, goblins and other supernatural beings was still prevalent among the scattered farming communities of the parish. Regarding the 'fairy-rings' near the head of Little Fryup Dale, one old man readily admitted that 'he and the other children of the hamlet used constantly to amuse themselves by running round and round these rings; but they had always been religiously careful never to run quite nine times round any one of them.' When asked why not?, he replied: 'Why sir, you see that if we had run the full number of nine times, that would have given the fairies power over us, and they would have come and taken us away for good, to go and live where they lived.'

'SPOUT HOUSE', BRANSDALE

In the remote moorland valley of Bransdale, west of Rudland Rigg, the farmhouses generally fall into two types: the adapted and converted longhouse, traditionally designed on a linear plan, with house, barn and byre under a single roof; and the two-storeyed, symmetrical building of the late eighteenth and early nineteenth century, with a central front door and rooms to either side. Spout House, the nearest farm in the photograph, is a good example of the latter, built when it was fashionable for yeoman farmers to copy the houses of the gentry. The farm building to the left (under the shadow of a tree) was built as a granary and cartshed: the former positioned above the latter to enable the air to circulate freely, thereby keeping the contents dry.

FARNDALE

Farndale – enfolded by the moorland heights of Rudland Rigg, Farndale Moor and Blakey Ridge – is a long, narrow, steep-sided valley famous for the wild, yellow daffodils that festoon the banks of the River Dove each spring. Known as Lenten Lilies, because they bloom around Easter time, the flowers were once in danger of being wiped out by irresponsible visitors. Now the plants are protected by law, and, since 1955, some 2,000 acres of the 'daffodil dale' has been designated as a nature reserve. The name 'Farndale' is generally thought to mean 'fern valley', but it may be derived from the Gaelic word for 'alder'. Although much of the dale is occupied by scattered farmsteads, it also contains three small but distinct hamlets – Church Houses, Low Mill and Lowna.

OLD RALPH CROSS, WESTERDALE MOOR

On Danby High Moor and Westerdale Moor, near the head of Rosedale, are two stone crosses bearing the same name – Old Ralph and Young Ralph. The former, and most ancient, cross is said to be named after a lay servant at the small Cistercian nunnery in Rosedale (founded some time before 1158). Young Ralph was erected near the site of an earlier boundary cross known as 'Crux Radulphi', and it is thought to date from the eighteenth century. At one time, it was the usual practice for travellers to place coins in the hollow found at the top of this nine-foot-high cross, but the practice ceased after the shaft was broken into three sections in 1961. In addition to being a prominent moorland landmark, standing at the geological centre of the North York Moors, Young Ralph was adopted as the emblem of the National Park in 1974.

FAT BETTY, DANBY HIGH MOOR

The most famous of all the hundreds of marker stones and crosses found scattered throughout the North York Moors is the group on Danby High Moor known as Fat Betty, Old Ralph, Young Ralph and the Margery Stone. According to legend, in order to settle a boundary dispute, Sister Elizabeth of Rosedale arranged to meet Sister Margery of Baysdale at a point midway between their two convents. Sister Elizabeth was escorted by Ralph, an elderly lay servant. Unfortunately, a thick fog descended on the moor and both parties became lost. Ralph set off to find Sister Margery, while Sister Elizabeth waited and prayed beside a large rock. When the fog eventually cleared, Sister Elizabeth spotted, in the distance, old Ralph and Sister Margery standing on two separate stones, not far from each other. The present stones are supposed to mark their respective positions.

DANBY HIGH MOOR

The expansive block of heather-
and bilberry-covered moorland
centred on Danby High Moor – some
1,400 feet above sea-level – is a main
watershed, with streams draining
north into the River Esk, to enter the
North Sea at Whitby; and south into
the River Derwent, a tributary of the
Ouse, to debouch into the Humber
at Hull. Radiating northward from
this central block, like the spokes
of a giant wheel, are a series of deep
valleys – Westerdale, Danby Dale,
Great Fryup Dale and Glaisdale.
Separating each of the dales is a
succession of descending ridges,
or 'riggs', on which evidence of
prehistoric occupation can be
found, including barrows, burial
mounds and rectangular enclosures.
A single standing stone on Danby
Rigg is all that survives of a Bronze
Age stone circle.

DANBY HEAD, DANBY HIGH MOOR

In *Forty Years in a Moorland Parish* the Rev. Atkinson characterized the North York Moors as a 'District of Surprises'. To discover the small, rather than grand, surprises he suggested that: '. . . one should prowl about on the rough braes of the broken moor-banks, and within the romantic fastnesses of the Dales Heads. Every twenty yards almost, as you wind in and out, climb up or climb down, some new feature, some new object, some new scene, something you would give much to be able to photograph on the instant, and carry away with you indelible forever, simply comes to be looked at; and, as you turn aside, or press farther on in your course, gives way to another, equally beautiful and equally desirable in its beauty. In one word, our moorland scenery needs to be lived among.'

SWALEDALE SHEEP, DANBY HIGH MOOR

In the North York Moors the most predominant sheep, reared for both meat and wool, is the Swaledale, one of the hardiest of breeds, easily recognized by its black face, white muzzle and speckled grey legs. Although Swaledales – both sexes of which are horned – have the protection of long, loose fleeces of coarse, white wool, additional much-needed shelter on the exposed moorland is provided by 'bields' or windbreaks of stone. Unfortunately, estimates suggest that careless drivers on the unfenced roads account for as many as ten per cent of moorland sheep deaths. A further threat to the livelihood of the farmer is the fact that over recent years sheep stealing (which has always been endemic because of the vastness and remoteness of the moors) has increased at an alarming rate.

LITTLE BLAKEY HOWE

According to age-old belief, many of the prehistoric monuments found scattered throughout the North York Moors were inhabited by fairies and hobgoblins (or hobs). Most of these sometimes helpful and sometimes mischievous little people also frequented the nearby dales. The hob known as Obtrusch, for example, lived in a tumulus of the same name on Rudland Rigg, but made life so unbearable for one Farndale farmer that the poor man decided to go and live elsewhere. 'Ah see thoo's flittin!', said a neighbour meeting the farmer on the road near Little Blakey Howe. 'Aye, we's flittin!' said a cheeky goblin's voice from somewhere inside the laden cart. Realizing that there was little point in leaving if the hob was to follow him, the farmer turned around and went back home.

BLAKEY RIDGE

The oldest routes across the North York Moors kept to the ridge-ways – high, firm ground above the dales. Many of these routes, like that running along Blakey Ridge, are marked by stones, variously called 'waymarkers', 'guidestones' and (for those carved with hands) 'hand-stones'. In addition to guide posts can be found standing stones, crosses, boundary markers, memorial stones, cairns, and what are simply recorded on the Ordnance Survey map (1:25 000) as 'piles of stones'. The road traversing Blakey Ridge leads south to Hutton-le-Hole, and north to Young Ralph Cross (from where there is a choice of routes north to Westerdale, Castleton and Esk Dale, and south-east to Rosedale). At the northern end of the ridge, near Blakey Howe, is the remote Lion Inn.

EAST MINES, ROSEDALE

Although iron ore had been mined in Rosedale from at least the Middle Ages, mining on an intensive scale did not begin until much more recently – the middle of the nineteenth century. After the opening in 1856 of the Hollins, or West, Mines, located about a mile south of Rosedale Abbey, the population of the dale increased dramatically (from 558 in 1851 to 2,839 just twenty years later in 1871). The opening of further mines, including the East Mines (on the east side of Rosedale), and the arrival of the railway in 1861 escalated the production of iron ore. It is said that there were so many miners in the 1870s, working shift after shift in the area, that 'the beds were never cold'. The end of ironstone mining in the dale was marked by the closure of the East Mines in 1926. In the photograph can be seen the remains of calcining kilns.

BOUNDARY STONE, BLAKEY RIDGE

Some of the stones marking the moorland boundaries of the Feversham estates bear the initials T. D., which stand for Thomas Duncombe of Duncombe Park, the ancestral home of the Earls of Feversham. It was Sir Charles Duncombe, a wealthy London goldsmith and banker, who purchased the Helmsley estates (including the castle) in 1689. After his sister, the wife of Thomas Browne, inherited the estates in 1711, she and her husband assumed the name of Duncombe. They (followed by their son, Thomas Duncombe II) built the original house at Duncombe Park (it was rebuilt after the disastrous fire of 1879 and is now open to the public). Thomas Duncombe III succeeded to the Feversham estates in 1746. At Helmsley there is a canopied monument to the 2nd Lord Feversham, who died in 1867.

ROSEDALE, FROM ROSEDALE HEAD

Unlike accidental fires, which get out of control and destroy not only the surface vegetation, but also the underlying peat, leaving a barren desert of gravelly rock, controlled burning of the heather moorland does not produce enough heat to kill the plant's roots. The soil is also preserved, because the burning, or 'swiddening', takes place between November and March when the peat is damp. Most of the uncontrolled moorland fires, which occur every year without fail, are caused by people being careless with matches, cigarette ends, picnic stoves and the like. In 1976, for example, more than sixty separate, uncontrolled fires destroyed eight square miles of heather moorland. Two penetrated so deep into the peat that it took three months before the fire was safely extinguished.

SPAUNTON MOOR, FROM SPINDLE THORN

Although grouse are found throughout the northern hemisphere, the red grouse (*Lagopus lagopus scoticus*) is unique to Britain. Its natural habitat is heather moorland, on which it remains all year, rarely venturing beyond its breeding area. It is said that almost all wild grouse die within a mile of the place in which they were reared. Landowners maintain the numbers of grouse on the moorland by managed breeding and the systematic burning of heather to encourage new growth (essential to the birds' survival). Yet, for reasons that cannot be agreed, the grouse population in Britain has almost halved since the 1970s. Beyond dispute is the fact that a significant proportion are killed during the grouse-shooting season (from August's 'Glorious Twelfth' to 10 December).

'BURNLEY HOUSE', HUTTON-LE-HOLE

Lying in a hollow at the southern edge of the North York Moors, overlooking the Vale of Pickering, the village of Hutton-le-Hole once belonged to the Benedictine monks of St Mary's Abbey at York. In the Domesday Book, it is simply recorded as 'Hotun', from the Old English for 'farm on or by a ridge'. Like 'Burnley House' (also known as 'Moorlands'), the oldest buildings are of cruck-frame construction. Most date from the seventeenth century when many of the Quaker families wove woollen cloth in their own homes. Rushing through the middle of the long, undulating village green, where grazing sheep keep the grass short, is the Hutton Beck. At the Ryedale Folk Museum (in the village) are many re-erected examples of traditional buildings, including a manor house, a crofter's cottage and a medieval longhouse.

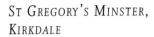

St Gregory's Minster, Kirkdale

From its source on the open, heather-clad moors, the Hodge Beck flows south-eastward through Bransdale and the deep wooded, limestone gorge of Kirk Dale to join the River Dove beyond Welburn. At Hole Cauldron, in Kirk Dale, the stream enters a subterranean tunnel eventually to re-emerge near Welburn Hall. After heavy rain or floods, some of the surplus water is carried along the surface bed and over the ford at Kirkdale (which during the summer is often dry). On the west bank of the beck, near the ford, stands the lonely and secluded church of St Gregory's Minster. Carved in a stone slab above the south doorway is a Saxon sundial with a short, but important, inscription dating the building to between 1055 and 1065. The small tower and chancel are nineteenth century.

Rievaulx Abbey

The remains of Rievaulx Abbey, the first Cistercian house in the north of England and one of the great mother churches of the Order in Britain, stand on the banks of the River Rye, a few miles upstream from Helmsley. 'Rievaulx' comes from a Franco-Norman word meaning 'valley of the Rye'. In the eighteenth century, the abbey ruins (now in the care of English Heritage) were a 'picturesque' feature in the landscaped walk known as Rievaulx Terrace and Temples (now owned by the National Trust). The terrace, with its two Grecian-style temples, was built on the thickly wooded hillside above the abbey ruins by Thomas Duncombe III, of nearby Duncombe Park, in 1758. His father created the older, more formal terrace and temples at Duncombe Park (also open to the public).

AMPLEFORTH ABBEY & COLLEGE

In 1793, the year France declared war on Britain, an English Benedictine community in Lorraine (with a direct connection with the monks that taught in the school attached to Westminster Abbey before the Dissolution) returned to England and, in 1802, settled at Ampleforth on the south-western fringe of the North York Moors. The original building was a small Georgian house built by the Fairfax family of nearby Gilling Castle. Today, in addition to the monastery and abbey church (designed by Sir Giles Gilbert Scott and built between 1922 and 1961), the monks run Ampleforth College, which is one of the leading Roman Catholic public schools in the country. Gilling Castle, acquired by the Community in 1929, was converted and is now the Ampleforth College Junior School.

LOW BRIDESTONES, GRIME MOOR

The outcrops of sedimentary rock, on Grime Moor, at the north-western edge of Dalby Forest, are known as the Bridestones and were bequeathed to the National Trust in 1944. Since 1966 they have been part of the a nature reserve. Made up of alternating layers of hard and softer sandstones, the rocks were fashioned into their present surreal shapes by the erosive action of the elements. They can be reached from Stain Dale (on the Forestry Commission's Dalby Forest Drive) by a circular walk that climbs high above Dove Dale. In fact, there are two sets of Bridestones – High and Low – situated on opposite sides the steeply sloping valley known as Bridestones Griff. Although the origin of the name Bridestones is uncertain, they may be connected with ancient fertility rites.

LASTINGHAM

According to Bede, when St Cedd, who was a Lindisfarne monk, founded a monastery at Lastingham in AD 654, he chose a site 'among high and remote hills which appeared more suitable for the haunts of robbers and the dens of wild beasts than habitations for men; so that, as Isaiah prophesied, "in the habitation of dragons, where each lay, shall be grass with reeds and rushes"; that is, the fruit of good works should spring up, where once dwelt beasts, or where lived men after the manner of beasts.' About 1,300 years ago, in 664, before the monastery was completed, St Cedd fell victim to the plague and was buried first outside the monastery walls and later inside the church. The present church, which was completed in 1228, incorporates part of the abbey church, started by Abbot Stephen of Whitby in 1078, but never finished.

HOLE OF HORCUM, LEVISHAM MOOR

Near Saltergate, on the western side of the main road from Whitby to Pickering, is the Hole of Horcum, or the 'Devil's Punchbowl' – a natural hollow excavated many thousands of years ago by Ice Age meltwaters and the erosive action of springs. Local tradition says that the 300-feet-deep depression was the work of the Devil, or the giant Wade (who was also credited with building 'Wade's Causeway', the Roman military road on Wheeldale Moor, three miles to the north-west). With regard to the Devil, he was supposed to have created the hollow by scooping out a handful of earth and throwing it across the moors (to form the 876-feet-high Blakey Topping, about a mile to the east). Apparently, the marks left by his fingers can still be seen on the slopes of the Hole.

SALTERGATE MOOR

Almost half of the 553-square-mile North York Moors National Park is open moorland. Since much of it is covered by wide expanses of heather, it is also the largest area of heather-covered upland in England. In fact, the moorland sustains three different types of heather: the most dominant being ling (*Calluna vulgaris*), which blossoms in August and September. In boggy areas, bell heather (*Erica cinerea*) is a useful indicator to walkers of firmer ground, since it grows on the driest tussocks. Cross-leaved heather (*Erica tetralix*), however, is only found in damp and wet areas. The growth of the heather is managed by controlled burning, or 'swiddening', which removes the old woody plants and encourages young green shoots – essential nourishment for both sheep and grouse.

LILLA CROSS, FYLINGDALES MOOR

Lilla Cross, possibly the oldest Christian monument in the north of England, is said to have been erected by Edwin, King of Northumbria. Tradition says that, in 626, Edwin was saved from assassination by one of his followers, Lilla, who sacrificed his own life in the process. Lilla was buried on the moors in a Bronze Age 'howe', or tumulus, and the place marked by the cross. In 1952, when Fylingdales Moor became a military training area, the cross was removed to Sil Howe (near the junction of the road from Beck Hole with that between Goathland and Sleights). It was re-erected on its present site in 1962. The nearby truncated 'pyramid' of the Fylingdales Early Warning Station was completed in 1992 and replaced the celebrated trio of giant 'golf balls'.

ELLER BECK, BECK HOLE

Rising on Allerston High Moor, the six-mile-long Eller Beck flows north-west, past Goathland, to join the West Beck, near the tiny hamlet of Beck Hole. After becoming the Murk Esk, the waters of both streams join the Esk near Grosmont. From Beck Hole, a path leads up the steep northern bank of the Eller Beck to a small waterfall, known as Thomason Foss. The railway line running along the valley was built in 1865 to avoid the dangerously steep incline at Beck Hole. In the valley of the West Beck, about a mile south of Beck Hole, is the seventy-feet-high Mallyan Spout waterfall. Although Beck Hole now consists of only half a dozen or so dwellings, in the mid-nineteenth century the settlement was a thriving mining community, with two blast furnaces and more than thirty stone cottages.

FALLING FOSS,
NEAR LITTLE BECK

From the tiny hamlet of Littlebeck, a walk of just over a mile threads up the wooded valley of the Little Beck – past evidence of abandoned jet and alum workings – to 'Midge Hall' and the Falling Foss waterfall. The May Beck, which plunges over the fifty-feet precipice of FallingFoss into the ravine of the Little Beck, rises on Sneaton High Moor (afforested by the Forestry Commission in 1968). From the May Beck car park (south of the Falling Foss car park), the May Beck Trail, established in 1973, follows a circular moorland-and-forest route of about three miles. Along the trail can be found the stone base of John Cross, reputedly named after Abbot John de Steyngrave of Whitby. The letter 'C', inscribed on the boundary marker now inserted in the ancient base, refers to the Cholmley estate.

'MIDGE HALL',
LITTLE BECK VALLEY

'Midge Hall', just above the Falling Foss waterfall, was once a gamekeeper's cottage, and later a museum. It was built in the early nineteenth century by the owner of the Sneaton estate, Sir James Wilson, who also built Sneaton Castle near Whitby. Traces of the Hall's outdoor toilet, which was strategically positioned almost over the fall, can still be found. The Hermitage, about three quarters of a mile down the Little Beck valley, was reputedly hollowed out of the sandstone rock by a mason called Jeffrey, who also carved two small seats on the top. Inscribed above the entrance is the date '1790' and the letters 'G. C.' – thought to refer to George Chubb, a schoolmaster from the hamlet of Littlebeck, who was involved in the building of nearby Newton House.

Robin Hood's Bay

Although there is no real evidence to connect Robin Hood's Bay with the legendary outlaw of the same name, local tradition maintains that he sought refuge in the area, and kept a boat in the bay, ready for a quick escape to sea. Details in the medieval ballads and stories of Robin Hood suggest that the popular hero, who took from the rich to give to the poor, had his origins in Yorkshire, rather than Nottingham. Indeed, in the fourteenth-century ballad *Robin Hood and Guy of Gisborne*, the outlaw identifies himself as 'Robin Hood of Barnsdale' (some eight miles north-west of Doncaster).

Later traditions locate his birthplace at Loxley (on the outskirts of Sheffield). Another ballad states that he died at Kirklees Priory (where, nearby, can be found the grave of a 'Roberd Hude.')

The Openings, Robin Hood's Bay

With its jumbled warren of steep alleyways, narrow passages and tightly packed houses rising up from cobbled roads, the fishing village of Robin Hood's Bay was once a notorious haven for smugglers. It is claimed that the contraband could be passed from from one end of the village to the other without appearing in the open.

In his 1914 *Guide to Robin Hoods' Bay*, the Rev. William Dalton wrote: 'The rocks and holds were full of "stow-holes", into which the cargo of a good-sized lugger could disappear upon emergency: and there was scarcely a house without its secret hiding places, or false masonry, or something of this kind . . . In this "trade" the townspeople were ably assisted by the farmers living in the country, and by the alum-workers at Peak and Stoupe Brow.'

ROBIN HOOD'S BAY

The oldest part of Robin Hood's Bay (also known as Bay Town, or simply Bay) lies at the foot of New Road, the steep main street leading down to the sea. Subsequent development higher up the slopes was brought about by increased wealth from the fishing industry and the arrival of the railway in 1885. Although some of the houses date from the seventeenth century, including the boyhood home of the novelist Leo Walmsley (1892–1966), most were built in the early eighteenth century. In 1780 part of King Street, the old main street, collapsed and slipped into the sea. Further cliff falls led to the building of the New Road. Before the construction of the 500-feet-long and 40-feet-high seawall in 1975, nearly 200 houses had been washed away.

SCARBOROUGH CASTLE

Excavation on the rocky headland separating Scarborough's North and South Bays has unearthed evidence of early Iron Age occupation, including the remains of wattle-and-daub huts. During Roman times the hill became the site of a signal station, one in a chain of similar stations set up along the coast to give warning of the approach of enemy ships. The first castle to stand on the headland was probably erected, early in the reign of King Stephen (1135–54), by William le Gros, Earl of Albermarle (and Earl of Yorkshire after 1138). It was a royal stronghold from the reign of Henry II (1154–89) to that of James I (1603–25), when (in a ruinous state) it was granted to John, Earl of Holderness. The castle suffered further damage during the Civil War and First World War.

PICKERING CASTLE

John Leland, the antiquarian, visited the market town of Pickering, at the southern edge of the North York Moors, in about 1540 and wrote in his *Itinerary*: 'the castle standeth in an end of the town not far from the parish church on the brow of the hill, under which the brook runneth. In the first court of it be a four towers, of which one is called Rosamund's Tower. In the inner court be also a four towers, whereof the keep is one. The castle walls and the towers be meetly well, the lodgings in the inner court that be of timber be in ruin.' The earthen motte-and-bailey castle was built by William the Conqueror, probably in 1069–70. Most of the present stone fortress (now in the care of English Heritage) dates from between 1180 and 1326.

LOW MOORS, VALE OF PICKERING

Stretching eastward from the Vale of York to the sea is the fertile plain of the Vale of Pickering, which is watered by several streams that rise on the heather-clad plateau of the North York Moors: the Seph, the Rye, the Hodge Beck, the Seven, the Derwent and the Dove. To the south of the moors lie the richly wooded Howardian Hills and the intensely farmed Wolds: one block of upland separated from the other by the valley of Derwent. Most of the dykes that drain the Vale of Pickering date from monastic times (for example, Friar Dyke at Wilton Carr). In *Britannia*, the antiquarian and historian William Camden wrote of the low-lying areas of the East Riding: 'That part of it towards the sea and the river Derwent is pretty fruitful; but the middle is nothing but a heap of mountains, called "Yorkeswold", which signifies "Yorkshire hills".'

VALE OF PICKERING, FROM THE WOLDS

Before the Ice Ages, the waters of the Vale of Pickering drained directly eastward into the sea. After the arrival of the ice, however, this exit was blocked, creating a vast meltwater lake, covering an area of over 160 square miles. At its western end, near Ampleforth, the water was trapped by the Vale of York glacier. It finally escaped by cutting its way through the hills south of Malton, and in the process created the gorges near Kirkham. All the streams that now flow through the rich, alluvial plain of the Vale of Pickering merge with the Derwent, a tributary of the Ouse. The Derwent's eastern exit into the North Sea was similarly blocked during the Ice Ages. In consequence, it carved a new route south through Forge Valley and west across the Vale of Pickering.

SHERIFF HUTTON CASTLE

Dominating the old market settlement of Sheriff Hutton, some ten miles north of York, are the remains of the castle founded in 1382 by John de Neville of Raby. Prior to the building of a motte-and-bailey castle on a nearby site by Bertram de Bulmer, Sheriff of York, in about 1140, the village was simply known as Hutton. The present castle, of which only the broken corner towers survive, was originally similar in design to the 'quadrangular palace castle' at Bolton, near Middleham. In about 1540 John Leland visited 'Shirhuten' and wrote of the castle: 'I saw no house in the north so like a princely lodgings. There is a park by the castle. This castle was well maintained by reason that the late Duke of Norfolk lay there ten years, and since the Duke of Richmond.'

CASTLE HOWARD,
NEAR MALTON

Described by Horace Walpole as 'a palace, a town, a fortified city', Castle Howard is attributed to three men: Charles Howard, 3rd Earl of Carlisle, Sir John Vanbrugh and Nicholas Hawksmoor. In 1698, Carlisle – having quarrelled with his first choice of architect – asked the dramatist John Vanbrugh to design him a new house. It was an unlikely, but inspired choice, for up to that point Vanbrugh's architectural experience was absolutely nil. Nevertheless, working closely with Hawksmoor, he created one of Yorkshire's largest and greatest houses. Work on the Baroque masterpiece began in 1700 and continued for more than fifty years. The house was finished by the 4th Earl's brother-in-law, Sir Thomas Robinson. The dome was destroyed by fire in 1940, and has since been rebuilt.

YORK MINSTER, FROM THE CITY WALLS

After the withdrawal of the Roman legions, Eboracum (York) became Eoforwic – the capital of the Anglo-Saxon kingdom of Northumbria. The first Minster, built of wood on the site of the former Roman Principia (military headquarters), was founded in the seventh century by Edwin, King of Northumbria. Shortly after, it was replaced by a cathedral of stone. Fire severely damaged the Anglo-Saxon building in 741, and destroyed it in 1069. In 1070, York's first Norman archbishop, Thomas of Bayeux, began the construction of a new cathedral in the Romanesque style. The present Minster, the fourth to stand on this same site, was built in the period between 1220 and 1480. The south transept was restored after being gutted by fire in 1984.

ST MARY'S ABBEY, YORK

Although famed for its magnificent cathedral, York – once an important port and trading centre on the River Ouse – contains many other places of interest, including the ruins of St Mary's Abbey, which was once one of the largest and wealthiest Benedictine houses in the north of the country. Originally founded before 1086 on a smaller site at nearby Marygate, the monastery was refounded on its present site, to the west of the Minster, in 1088. The community came to York from Whitby Abbey by way of Lastingham. A dispute over the slackening of the Rule in 1132 led to the founding of Fountains Abbey by a reformist group of monks from St Mary's. After the Dissolution, the stone from the abbey was used for many city buildings, notably in the rebuilding of St Olave's Church, Marygate.

CLIFFORD'S TOWER, YORK

After the Conquest of 1066, the victorious Normans built two motte-and-bailey castles at York – one at Baile Hill on the west bank of the River Ouse, followed by another on the east bank, where Clifford's Tower now stands. The second fortification was constructed shortly after most of the city, including the Minster, was destroyed during the Anglo-Danish-Scottish insurrection of 1069. In 1190 members of the York Jewish community were besieged in the wooden keep, which originally stood on top of the high, conical mound. Those who did not die in the flames that consumed the structure, were murdered by the violent mob. The present tower (all that remains of the royal castle started by Henry III) is said to be named after Sir Roger Clifford, who was hung in chains from the walls in 1322.

TREASURER'S HOUSE, YORK

The Treasurer's House (now owned by the National Trust) and Gray's Court (now housing the History Department of the University College of Ripon and York St John) were originally parts of one large mansion, dating essentially from the late sixteenth and early seventeenth centuries. The former property is so-named because the earliest recorded house to stand on the site was the residence (from about 1100 until the Dissolution, when the office was abolished) of the treasurers of York Minster. After acquiring the building in 1897, Frank Green, a wealthy industrialist, engaged Temple Moore to restore and remodel it (Moore also restored Gray's Court for Edwin Gray). The formal walled garden was established by Green.

St William's College, York

The timber-framed building of St William's College, in College Street, was constructed in the 1460s to house the chantry priests of the nearby Minster. Above the doorway, between the street and the inner courtyard, is the seated figure of St William (William FitzHerbert, Archbishop of York in 1141–47 and 1153–54). The doors, however, are of twentieth-century origin and bear the carved mouse trademark of Robert Thompson of Kilburn. After the Dissolution, the building became a private house, and for nearly six months in 1642 it was the location of the printing press of Charles I (it was in York that the king briefly set up his base, prior to the outbreak of the Civil War). In 1899 the house was purchased by Frank Green and was subsequently extensively restored by architect Temple Moore. It now in the care of the Dean and Chapter of York.

KIRKHAM PRIORY

By the banks of the River Derwent, some five miles south-west of Malton, Kirkham Priory was founded for Augustinian canons in about 1122 by Walter l'Espec, Lord of Helmsley. Tradition says that it was built to commemorate his only son, Walter, who was killed in a horse-riding accident. L'Espec also founded the Cistercian abbey at Rievaulx in 1131. Although the early records show that the canons at Kirkham considered joining the new Cistercian order, the priory remained Augustinian until its dissolution in 1539. Among the remains, which are now in the care of English Heritage, is a magnificent, late-thirteenth-century gatehouse,

which is decorated with carved sculptures and the heraldic shields of its founder and patrons, the lords of Helmsley Castle.

DESERTED MEDIEVAL VILLAGE, WHARRAM PERCY

In a deep, sheltered dale, at the eastern edge of the Wolds, south of Settrington, lies Wharram Percy and the best-preserved ruins of a deserted medieval village in Britain (now in the care of English Heritage). It is one of over 3,000 Deserted Medieval Villages to have been discovered from traces of foundations and walls. Of these, over 370 have been identified in Yorkshire alone. The remains of the medieval parish church of St Martin, north of the millpond, can be seen in the photograph. Originally much larger, the church was reduced in size as the number of parishioners shrank. Most of the villages were depopulated during the fifteenth century, when the prosperity of the wool trade was at its peak, and landowners were eager to convert arable land to sheep pasture.

THE WOLDS,
FROM SETTRINGTON BEACON

Sweeping in a great crescent from the River Humber in the south to the cliffs of Flamborough Head in the east, the chalk hills of the Yorkshire Wolds attain a maximum height of 808 feet at Garrowby Top, not far from Bishop Wilton. Once used as meadows on which countless sheep grazed, their transformation into arable farmland began towards the end of the eighteenth century, when a number of landowners planted hedges to make large fields, and trees to provide shelter from the bitter North Sea winds. Although the downs are peppered with small villages and hamlets, the largest towns – and the so-called 'Capital of the Wolds', Great Driffield – lie on the edge of the chalk downs, not actually on them. The Wolds Way, a path opened up in 1982, runs from Hessle Haven on the River Humber to Filey Brigg – a distance of seventy-nine miles.

ALL SAINTS CHURCH, RUDSTON

In the graveyard of All Saints Church, in the Wolds village of Rudston, six miles west of Bridlington, stands a gigantic monolith, reputedly weighing over forty tons. Although it protrudes some twenty-six feet out of the ground, the stone's total length may be as much as forty-two feet, and possibly more. According to one legend, the Devil threw it dart-like at the church, but missed. Another says that it simply fell out of the sky killing certain people who were desecrating the churchyard. The gritstone monolith, the tallest standing stone in Britain, is thought to have been brought from Cayton Bay, near Scarborough, and erected in the late Neolithic period, presumably on a sacred site. The church was intentionally built right next to it in Norman times.

FILEY BRIGG

Filey Brigg – the slender mile-long promontory that shoots out into the sea from the high headland of Carr Naze, just north of the coastal resort of Filey – marks the end of both the 108-mile Cleveland Way and seventy-nine-mile Wolds Way. At low tide it is possible to walk along the Brigg, but it should be avoided in bad weather. Legend says that the natural breakwater was begun by the Devil in an abandoned attempt to build a road across the sea to Norway. Geologists, however, maintain that it is composed of hard Lower Calcareous Grit, which has been exposed by the erosive action of the waves. The softer boulder clay of the cliffs, deposited by the action of glaciers, has been sculpted into a dramatic assortment of sharp ridges and deep furrows.

BEMPTON CLIFFS, NEAR FLAMBOROUGH

In *The Coastline of England and Wales*, first published in 1946, J. A. Steers felt that the chalk cliffs eastward from Filey were equal to, or better than, those of the same type found elsewhere in England: 'Moreover, the details dependent on the boulder-clay covering of the Chalk at Flamborough add something which is necessarily absent from most of our Chalk cliffs. The natural setting of Thornwick and North Sea Landing is beautiful: they must be visited before the way in which man can spoil them is fully realised.' Bempton Cliffs, which are north-west of Flamborough Head, is now an RSPB reserve, and the breeding-ground of Britain's only mainland colony of gannets. Rising 400 feet from the North Sea, they are the highest chalk cliffs in England.

FLAMBOROUGH HEAD

The great chalk outcrop that runs north-east across England from Dorset – through Wessex, the Chilterns, East Anglia and the Yorkshire Wolds – terminates in the cliffs at Flamborough Head. From Wessex, it should be noted, long chalk limbs form the North and South Downs of south-east England. Interestingly, Flamborough's northern cliffs contain flints, while those to the south do not. The ceaseless onslaught of the waves has carved inlets, caves and pinnacles out of the face of the cliffs. In spring and early summer, vast numbers of sea birds nest on ledges and in crevices in the chalk. Usually they make their nests out of natural materials. But, occasionally, a bird will use convenient manufactured objects, such as the car tyre in the photograph!

LIGHTHOUSE, FLAMBOROUGH HEAD

Eighty-eight feet tall, the Flamborough Head lighthouse was built in 1806 by John Matson of Bridlington and designed by the architect Samuel Wyatt. An earlier coal-fired lighthouse (taking the form of an octagonal stone tower), stands about a quarter-of-a-mile further inland. It was built in about 1674 by Sir John Clayton. Near Matson's lighthouse is a toposcope (a squat pillar indicating compass points and the direction of local landmarks), erected in 1959 to commemorate the 1779 naval battle of Flamborough Head. In the battle, the British under Captain Robert Pearson were defeated by the Scots-born American privateer, John Paul Jones. Jones' flagship, the *Bonhomme Richard*, was so badly damaged, however, that it had to be abandoned and it subsequently sank.

North Sea,
from Yorkshire Coast

It is eastward to the North Sea that almost all the rivers of old Yorkshire turn. The Swale, Ure, Nidd, Wharfe, Aire, Don and Derwent join with the Ouse to debouch into the Humber. The Balder, Greta and Lune combine with the Tees to pour into Tees Bay. Between Humber and Tees, the Esk flows into Whitby harbour, and the Gypsey Race into Bridlington Bay. The waters of other, lesser rivers also find their way to the coast – where freshwater meets salt, and the age-old battle between land and sea is fought relentlessly (the latter drastically and continually redefining the former). Yet the North Sea is as much a part of Yorkshire as the land: both are exploited by man; both are rich in history and traditions; and both have inspired artists, writers and poets down the ages.

The North York Moors

The North York Moors National Park embraces a thirty-five-mile-wide upland swathe of wild heather moorland, cut by rich, green valleys and deep, dramatic ravines. Designated in 1952 and covering an area of 553 square miles, the Park is bounded to the east by the spectacular cliffs of the North Sea coast and to the west by the steep escarpments of the Cleveland and Hambleton Hills. To the south and west, respectively, the 1,400-feet-high moorland mass is bordered by the flat, fertile lowlands of the Vale of Pickering and the Vale of York. To the north and north-west are the level expanses of the Cleveland Plain and the Vale of Mowbray. The Park is criss-crossed by roads, tracks and paths, some of which date back to prehistoric times. The Romans constructed a road across Wheeldale Moor to their base at Cawthorn Camps, near Pickering. While stone-paved causeways were used by the medieval monks to transport coal, charcoal, ironstone, lime, wool and cloth across the marshy ground. Abbeys such as Gisborough, Rosedale and Rievaulx, as well as such castles as Helmsley and Pickering, were all linked by these moorland routes, many of which are still marked by stone crosses. The 100-mile Cleveland Way is one of a number of long-distance walks based in or around the Park. Most of the Park is in private ownership. However, the National Park Authority has acquired only 0.6 per cent of the total; the National Trust 1.2 per cent; and the Forestry Commission about 16.5 per cent, including Dalby Forest. The emblem adopted by the North Yorks National Park is the nine-feet-high Young Ralph Cross, on Westerdale Moor.

The Yorkshire Dales

Stretching for some thirty miles, between the wild moorland chain of the Pennines – the backbone of northern England – and the level plain of the Vale of York, the Yorkshire Dales National Park covers an area of 680 square miles. Established in 1954, the Park contains a rich variety of landscape: from lush green valleys, criss-crossed by mile after mile of drystone walling, to spectacular limestone pavements, soaring crags and dramatic scars. The limestone scenery of the southern Dales, which includes the great amphitheatre of Malham Cove and the precipitous cliffs of Gordale Scar, is not restricted to surface features alone. Underlying almost every hill is a honeycomb of subterranean passages, pot-holes and caverns, formed by the dissolving action of underground streams. The North Pennine cave area is Britain's largest and contains the internationally famed Gaping Gill pothole, into which a stream (Fell Beck) plunges 365 feet, down a vertical shaft and into a gigantic cathedral-sized chamber. Ingleborough (2,373 feet), Whernside (2,419 feet) and Pen-y-ghent (2,273 feet), three of Yorkshire's highest summits, lie within the Park and form the basis of the twenty-four-mile Three Peaks Walk. About a fifth of the 270-mile-long Pennine Way, passes through the Park, crossing the boundary near Gargrave in the south and Tan Hill in the north. Another popular long-distance route, which links the Lakes, Moors and Dales, is the 190-mile Coast to Coast Walk, devised by Alfred Wainwright (1906-91). As is the case with all Britain's National Parks, nearly all of the land in the Dales is privately owned. The National Park Authority has acquired only 0.1 per cent of the total and the National Trust 2.5 per cent. The emblem of the Yorkshire Dales National Park is the head of a Swaledale ram.

SELECTED PROPERTIES & REGIONAL OFFICES

North York Moors National Park

THE OLD VICARAGE
Bondgate
Helmsley
York YO6 5BP
Telephone: (01439) 770657

Yorkshire Dales National Park Authority

COLVEND
Hebden Road
Grassington
Skipton BD23 5LB
Telephone (01756) 752748

English Heritage

HISTORIC PROPERTIES NORTH
Bessie Surtees House
41-44 Sandhill
Newcastle-upon-Tyne NE1 3JF
Telephone: (0191) 2611585

BYLAND ABBEY
near Coxwold
North Yorkshire YO6 4BD
Open: daily end March to end October.
Telephone: (01347) 868614

CLIFFORD'S TOWER
Tower Street
York YO1 1SA
Open: daily throughout year, except Christmas.
Telephone: (01904) 646940

EASBY ABBEY
near Richmond
North Yorkshire
Open: daily at any reasonable time.

EGGLESTONE ABBEY
near Barnard Castle
County Durham
Open: daily at any reasonable time.

HELMSLEY CASTLE
Helmsley
York YO6 5AB
Open: daily throughout year, except Christmas.
Telephone: (01439) 770442

KIRKHAM PRIORY
Whitwell-on-the-Hill
York YO6 7JS
Open: daily end March to end September.
Telephone: (01653) 618768

MIDDLEHAM CASTLE
Middleham
Leyburn
North Yorkshire D48 4RJ
Open: daily end March to end October; Wednesdays to Sundays, November to end March; closed Christmas.
Telephone: (01969) 623899

MOUNT GRACE PRIORY
Osmotherley
Northallerton DL6 3JG
Open: daily end March to end October; Wednesdays to Sundays, November to end March; closed Christmas.
Telephone: (01609) 883494

PICKERING CASTLE
Pickering
York YO18 7AX
Open: daily end March to end October; Wednesdays to Sundays, November to end March; closed Christmas.
Telephone: (01751) 474989

RICHMOND CASTLE
Richmond
North Yorkshire DL10 4QW
Open: daily throughout year, except Christmas.
Telephone: (01748) 822493

RIEVAULX ABBEY
Rievaulx
Helmsley
York YO6 5LB
Open: daily throughout year, except Christmas.
Telephone: (01439) 798228

SCARBOROUGH CASTLE
Castle Road
Scarborough
North Yorkshire YO1 1HY
Open: daily end March to end October; Wednesdays to Sundays, November to end March; closed Christmas.
Telephone: (01723) 372451

WHARRAM PERCY DESERTED MEDIEVAL VILLAGE
Wharram-le-Street
North Yorkshire
Open: daily at any reasonable time.

WHITBY ABBEY
Whitby
North Yorkshire YO22 4JT
Open: daily throughout year; except Christmas.
Telephone: (01947) 603568

National Trust

YORKSHIRE REGIONAL OFFICE
27 Tadcaster Road
Dringhouses
York YO2 2QG
Telephone: (01904) 702021

FOUNTAINS ABBEY & STUDLEY ROYAL
Fountains
Ripon HG4 3DY
Open: Abbey & Gardens all year, except Christmas & Fridays from November to January; Deer Park open all year.
Telephone: (01765) 608888/601005

RIEVAULX TERRACE & TEMPLES
Rievaulx
Helmsley
York YO6 5LJ
Open: daily end March to end October.
Telephone: (01439) 798340

TREASURER'S HOUSE
Chapter Street
York YO1 2JD
Open: daily end March to end October.
Telephone: (01904) 624247

Miscellaneous

AMPLEFORTH ABBEY & COLLEGE
Ampleforth
York YO6 4EY
Telephone: (01439) 766764

BOLTON ABBEY
Estate Office
Bolton Abbey
Skipton BD23 6EX
Open: daily throughout year.
Telephone: (01756) 710227

BRONTË PARSONAGE MUSEUM
Haworth
Keighley
West Yorkshire BD22 8DR
Open: daily throughout year; except Christmas & mid January to early February.
Telephone: (01535) 642323

CASTLE HOWARD
near York
North Yorkshire YO6 7DA
Open: daily Easter to end October.
Telephone: (01653) 648444

DUNCOMBE PARK
Helmsley
York YO6 5EB
Open: House & Garden, March, April & November, Sundays to Thursdays; May to September, Sundays to Fridays.
Telephone: (01439) 770213

HAREWOOD HOUSE TRUST LTD.
Moorhouse
The Harewood Estate
Leeds
West Yorkshire LS17 9LQ
Open: daily mid March to end October.
Telephone: (0113) 2886331

PHOTOGRAPHIC INFORMATION

The Photographic information refers to: make and type of camera; film size; film stock (all Fuji); tripod or handheld; lens; f-stop; shutter speed; polarizing filter (if used).

All lenses had a filter attached primarily to protect the front element, but chosen to have a slight warming quality. The tripod was an amazingly light, but very strong, carbon-fibre Gitzo, and the light meter a handheld Seconic. All equipment was carried in standard rucksacks. The processing was by Colab, Coventry.

1 Nikon F3; 35mm; Velvia; handheld; 180mm; f5.6; 1/125sec

2 Fuji GX680; 6x8cm; Velvia; Tripod; 65mm; f22; 1/15sec

8–9 Hasselblad 503CX; 6x6cm; Provia; Tripod; 50mm; f22; 1/15sec

12 Hasselblad 503CX; 6x6cm; Provia; Tripod; 50mm; f22; 1/4sec; polarizer

16 Nikon F3; 35mm; Velvia; handheld; 35mm; f5.6; 1/125sec

16–7 Fuji GX680; 6x8cm; Velvia; Tripod; 65mm; f22; 1/4sec

18 Hasselblad 503CX; 6x6cm; Provia; Tripod; 150mm; f8; 1sec

19 Hasselblad 503CX; 6x6cm; Provia; Tripod; 50mm; f22; 1/4sec; polarizer

20 Hasselblad 503CX; 6x6cm; Provia; Tripod; 50mm; f22; 1/4sec; polarizer

21 Nikon F3; 35mm; Velvia; handheld; 35mm; f5.6; 1/60sec; polarizer

22–3 Fuji GX680; 6x8cm; Velvia; Tripod; 80mm; f22; 1/4sec

26–7 Hasselblad 503CX; 6x6cm; Provia; Tripod; 50mm; f22; 1/15sec

28 Nikon F3; 35mm; Velvia; handheld; 85mm; f8; 1/60sec

29 Nikon F3; 35mm; Velvia; handheld; 180mm; f5.6; 1/125sec

30 Nikon F3; 35mm; Velvia; handheld; 35mm; f8; 1/60sec; polarizer

30–1 Hasselblad 503CX; 6x6cm; Provia; Tripod; 50mm; f22; 1/2sec

32 Hasselblad 503CX; 6x6cm; Provia; Tripod; 80mm; f22; 1/15sec

33 (top) Nikon F3; 35mm; Velvia; handheld; 28mmPC; f8; 1/60sec

33 (bottom) Hasselblad 503CX; 6x6cm; Provia; Tripod; 50mm; f22; 1/15sec

34 (top) Nikon F3; 35mm; Velvia; handheld; 28mmPC; f8; 1/60sec

34 (bottom) Hasselblad 503CX; 6x6cm; Provia; Tripod; 80mm; f22; 1/4sec

35 Fuji GX680; 6x8cm; Velvia; Tripod; 65mm; f22; 1/2sec

36 (top) Fuji GX680; 6x8cm; Velvia; Tripod; 300mm; f22; 1/8sec

36 (bottom) Nikon F3; 35mm; Velvia; Tripod; 180mm; f22; 1/15sec

37 Hasselblad 503CX; 6x6cm; Provia; Tripod; 80mm; f22; 1/8sec; polarizer

38 Fuji GX680; 6x8cm; Velvia; Tripod; 65mm; f22; 1/8sec

38–9 Fuji GX680; 6x8cm; Velvia; Tripod; 300mm; f32; 1/2sec; polarizer

40 Fuji GX680; 6x8cm; Velvia; Tripod; 300mm; f22; 1/8sec

40–1 Fuji GX680; 6x8cm; Velvia; Tripod; 65mm; f22; 1/8sec

42–3 Fuji GX680; 6x8cm; Velvia; Tripod; 65mm; f22; 1/8sec; polarizer

43 Fuji GX680; 6x8cm; Velvia; Tripod; 65mm; f22; 1/4sec; polarizer

44 Fuji GX680; 6x8cm; Velvia; Tripod; 65mm; f22; 1sec

44–5 Fuji GX680; 6x8cm; Velvia; Tripod; 300mm; f22; 1/15sec

46 (top) Fuji GX680; 6x8cm; Velvia; Tripod; 210mm; f22; 1/2sec

46 (bottom) Nikon F3; 35mm; Velvia; handheld; 24mm; f8; 1/60sec

47 Fuji GX680; 6x8cm; Velvia; Tripod; 65mm; f22; 1/15sec

48 Fuji GX680; 6x8cm; Velvia; Tripod; 65mm; f22; 1/4sec; polarizer

49 Fuji GX680; 6x8cm; Velvia; Tripod; 65mm; f22; 1/4sec; polarizer

50–1 Fuji GX680; 6x8cm; Velvia; Tripod; 80mm; f22; 1/8sec

51 Fuji GX680; 6x8cm; Velvia; Tripod; 65mm; f22; 1/4sec

52 Fuji GX680; 6x8cm; Velvia; Tripod; 65mm; f22; 1/8sec

52–3 Fuji GX680; 6x8cm; Velvia; Tripod; 65mm; f22; 1/8sec

54–5 Fuji GX680; 6x8cm; Velvia; Tripod; 210mm; f22; 1/15sec

55 Fuji GX680; 6x8cm; Velvia; Tripod; 210mm; f22; 1/8sec

56 Nikon F3; 35mm; Velvia; handheld; 180mm; f5.6; 1/125sec

57 (top) Nikon F3; 35mm; Velvia; handheld; 24mm; f5.6; 1/60sec

57 (bottom) Pentax 6x7; Fuji50; Tripod; 200mm; f22; 1/2se

58–9 Fuji GX680; 6x8cm; Velvia; Tripod; 210mm; f22; 1/8sec

60 (top) Nikon F3; 35mm; Velvia; handheld; 85mm; f8; 1/60sec

60 (bottom) Hasselblad 503CX; 6x6cm; Provia; Tripod; 80mm; f22; 1/4sec; polarizer

60–1 Fuji GX680; 6x8cm; Velvia; Tripod; 65mm; f22; 1/15sec

62 Hasselblad 503CX; 6x6cm; Provia; Tripod; 150mm; f22; 1/15sec

63 Fuji GX680; 6x8cm; Velvia; Tripod; 300mm; f22; 1/8sec

64 Fuji GX680; 6x8cm; Velvia; Tripod; 80mm; f22; 1/8sec

64–5 Fuji GX680; 6x8cm; Velvia; Tripod; 65mm; f22; 1/2sec; polarizer

66–7 Hasselblad 503CX; 6x6cm; Provia; Tripod; 150mm; f16; 1/30sec

67 (top) Hasselblad 503CX; 6x6cm; Provia; Tripod; 50mm; f22; 1/4sec; polarizer

67 (bottom) Fuji GX680; 6x8cm; Velvia; Tripod; 210mm; f22; 1/8sec

68 (top) Hasselblad 503CX; 6x6cm; Provia; Tripod; 150mm; f22; 1/4sec; polarizer

68 (bottom) Nikon F3; 35mm; Velvia; handheld; 35mm; f8; 1/60sec

69 Hasselblad 503CX; 6x6cm; Provia; Tripod; 80mm; f22; 1/4sec; polarizer

70 Hasselblad 503CX; 6x6cm; Provia; Tripod; 150mm; f22; 1/15sec

71 (top) Hasselblad 503CX; 6x6cm; Provia; Tripod; 80mm; f22; 1/4sec; polarizer

71 (bottom) Nikon F3; 35mm; Velvia; handheld; 28mmPC; f8; 1/60sec

72 Hasselblad 503CX; 6x6cm; Provia; Tripod; 80mm; f22; 1/4sec; polarizer

73 (top) Nikon F3; 35mm; Velvia; handheld; 28mmPC; f8; 1/60sec

73 (middle) Nikon F3; 35mm; Velvia; handheld; 24mm; f8; 1/60sec

73 (bottom) Nikon F3; 35mm; Velvia; handheld; 24mm; f5.6; 1/30sec; polarizer

74 Fuji GX680; 6x8cm; Velvia; Tripod; 65mm; f22; 1/8sec

75 Fuji GX680; 6x8cm; Velvia; Tripod; 210mm; f22; 1/8sec

76 (top) Nikon F3; 35mm; Velvia; handheld; 28mmPC; f8; 1/60sec

76 (bottom) Nikon F3; 35mm; Velvia; handheld; 28mmPC; f8; 1/30sec

76–7 Nikon F3; 35mm; Velvia; handheld; 85mm; f5.6; 1/60sec

78–9 Hasselblad 503CX; 6x6cm; Provia; Tripod; 80mm; f22; 1/4sec; polarizer

79 Nikon F3; 35mm; Velvia; handheld; 28mmPC; f8; 1/60sec

80–1 Fuji GX680; 6x8cm; Velvia; Tripod; 300mm; f22; 1/8sec

82–3 Fuji GX680; 6x8cm; Velvia; Tripod; 300mm; f22; 1/8sec

83 Fuji GX680; 6x8cm; Velvia; Tripod; 65mm; f22; 1/8sec

84–5 Fuji GX680; 6x8cm; Velvia; Tripod; 65mm; f22; 1/8scc

85 (top) Nikon F3; 35mm; Velvia; handheld; 28mmPC; f8; 1/60sec

85 (bottom) Nikon F3; 35mm; Velvia; handheld; 28mmPC; f8; 1/60sec

86 Hasselblad 503CX; 6x6cm; Provia; Tripod; 80mm; f22; 1/4sec; polarizer

86–7 Hasselblad 503CX; 6x6cm; Provia; Tripod; 80mm; f22; 1/4sec; polarizer

88 (top) Hasselblad 503CX; 6x6cm; Provia; Tripod; 150mm; f11; 1sec

88 (bottom) Hasselblad 503CX; 6x6cm; Provia; Tripod; 80mm; f22; 1/15sec

89 Hasselblad 503CX; 6x6cm; Provia; Tripod; 150mm; f22; 1/15sec

90 Fuji GX680; 6x8cm; Velvia; Tripod; 80mm; f22; 1/8sec

90–1 Fuji GX680; 6x8cm; Velvia; Tripod; 210mm; f22; 1/8sec

92–3 Fuji GX680; 6x8cm; Velvia; Tripod; 210mm; f22; 1/8sec

93 Fuji GX680; 6x8cm; Velvia; Tripod; 65mm; f22; 1/2sec

94–5 Pentax 6x7; Fuji50; Tripod; 200mm; f22; 1sec

96–7 Fuji GX680; 6x8cm; Velvia; Tripod; 65mm; f22; 1/2sec; polarizer

97 Nikon F3; 35mm; Velvia; handheld; 28mmPC; f8; 1/60sec

98–9 Pentax 6x7; Fuji50; Tripod; 75mm; f22; 1/15sec

99 Hasselblad 503CX; 6x6cm; Provia; Tripod; 50mm; f22; 1/5sec

100 Hasselblad 503CX; 6x6cm; Provia; Tripod; 150mm; f11; 1sec

100–1 Fuji GX680; 6x8cm; Velvia; Tripod; 300mm; f22; 4sec

102 Hasselblad 503CX; 6x6cm; Provia; Tripod; 50mm; f22; 1/8sec

103 Nikon F3; 35mm; Velvia; handheld; 24mm; f8; 1/60sec

104 (top) Hasselblad 503CX; 6x6cm; Provia; Tripod; 50mm; f22; 1/4sec; polarizer

104 (bottom) Nikon F3; 35mm; Velvia; handheld; 24mm; f8; 1/60sec

105 Pentax 6x7; Fuji50; Tripod; 200mm; f22; 1/2sec

106–7 Pentax 6x7; Fuji50; Tripod; 45mm; f22; 1/2sec; polarizer

107 Pentax 6x7; Fuji50; Tripod; 45mm; f22; 1/2sec; polarizer

108 Nikon F3; 35mm; Velvia; handheld; 180mm; f5.6; 1/250sec

109 Nikon F3; 35mm; Velvia; handheld; 24mm; f8; 1/60sec

110 (top) Hasselblad 503CX; 6x6cm; Provia; Tripod; 80mm; f22; 1/4sec; polarizer

110 (bottom) Hasselblad 503CX; 6x6cm; Provia; Tripod; 80mm; f22; 1/4sec; polarizer

110–1 Fuji GX680; 6x8cm; Velvia; Tripod; 65mm; f22; 1/8sec

112 Hasselblad 503CX; 6x6cm; Provia; Tripod; 50mm; f22; 1/4sec; polarizer

113 Hasselblad 503CX; 6x6cm; Provia; Tripod; 65mm; f22; 1/4sec; polarizer

114–5 Pentax 6x7; Fuji50; Tripod; 75mm; f22; 1/4sec; polarizer

116–7 Pentax 6x7; Fuji50; Tripod; 45mm; f22; 1/2sec; polarizer

117 Nikon F3; 35mm; Velvia; handheld; 85mm; f5.6; 1/125sec

118 Pentax 6x7; Fuji50; Tripod; 45mm; f22; 1/4sec; polarizer

118–9 Fuji GX680; 6x8cm; Velvia; Tripod; 65mm; f22; 1/4sec; polarizer

120 Hasselblad 503CX; 6x6cm; Provia; Tripod; 50mm; f22; 1/15sec

120–1 Pentax 6x7; Fuji50; Tripod; 45mm; f22; 1/15sec

122 Hasselblad 503CX; 6x6cm; Provia; Tripod; 50mm; f22; 1/15sec

122–3 Pentax 6x7; Fuji50; Tripod; 45mm; f22; 1/8sec

124 Nikon F3; 35mm; Velvia; handheld; 35mm; f8; 1/30sec; polarizer

125 (top) Nikon F3; 35mm; Velvia; handheld; 28mmPC; f5.6; 1/60sec

125 (bottom) Nikon F3; 35mm; Velvia; handheld; 28mmPC; f8; 1/60sec

126 (top) Nikon F3; 35mm; Velvia; handheld; 28mmPC; f8; 1/60sec

126 (bottom) Hasselblad 503CX; 6x6cm; Provia; Tripod; 50mm; f22; 1/4sec; polarizer

127 Hasselblad 503CX; 6x6cm; Provia; Tripod; 150mm; f22; 1/15sec

128–9 Hasselblad 503CX; 6x6cm; Provia; Tripod; 80mm; f22; 1/15sec

129 Nikon F3; 35mm; Velvia; handheld; 85mm; f5.6; 1/125sec

130 Pentax 6x7; Fuji50; Tripod; 45mm; f22; 1/2sec; polarizer

130–1 Pentax 6x7; Fuji50; Tripod; 45mm; f22; 1sec

132 Fuji GX680; 6x8cm; Velvia; Tripod; 210mm; f22; 1sec

132–3 Hasselblad 503CX; 6x6cm; Provia; Tripod; 80mm; f22; 1/15sec

134–5 Hasselblad 503CX; 6x6cm; Provia; Tripod; 150mm; f22; 1/15sec

135 Nikon F3; 35mm; Velvia; handheld; 24mm; f8; 1/60sec

136–7 Pentax 6x7; Fuji50; Tripod; 45mm; f22; 1/2sec; polarizer

137 Nikon F3; 35mm; Velvia; handheld; 28mmPC; f8; 1/60sec

138 Pentax 6x7; Fuji50; Tripod; 45mm; f22; 1/2sec; polarizer

139 Pentax 6x7; Fuji50; Tripod; 45mm; f22; 1/2sec; polarizer

140 (top) Hasselblad 503CX; 6x6cm; Provia; Tripod; 80mm; f22; 1/2sec; polarizer

140 (bottom) Nikon F3; 35mm; Velvia; handheld; 28mmPC; f8; 1/60sec

141 Nikon F3; 35mm; Velvia; handheld; 24mm; f5.6; 1/30sec; polarizer

142–3 Hasselblad 503CX; 6x6cm; Provia; Tripod; 50mm; f22; 1/2sec; polarizer

143 Nikon F3; 35mm; Velvia; handheld; 28mmPC; f8; 1/60sec

144 (top) Nikon F3; 35mm; Velvia; handheld; 28mmPC; f8; 1/60sec

144 (bottom) Nikon F3; 35mm; Velvia; handheld; 28mmPC; f8; 1/60sec

145 Nikon F3; 35mm; Velvia; handheld; 28mmPC; f8; 1/60sec

146 (top) Nikon F3; 35mm; Velvia; handheld; 28mmPC; f8; 1/60sec

146 (bottom) Fuji GX680; 6x8cm; Velvia; Tripod; 65mm; f22; 1/8sec

147 Hasselblad 503CX; 6x6cm; Provia; Tripod; 50mm; f22; 1/4sec; polarizer

148 Nikon F3; 35mm; Velvia; handheld; 28mmPC; f8; 1/60sec

148–9 Hasselblad 503CX; 6x6cm; Provia; Tripod; 50mm; f22; 1/15sec

149 Hasselblad 503CX; 6x6cm; Provia; Tripod; 80mm; f22; 1/15sec

150 Hasselblad 503CX; 6x6cm; Provia; Tripod; 80mm; f11; 1/60sec

150–1 Hasselblad 503CX; 6x6cm; Provia; Tripod; 50mm; f22; 1/2scc; polarizer

152–3 Nikon F3; 35mm; Velvia; handheld; 85mm; f5.6; 1/60sec

Drystone Walls
The photographs of drystone walls which appear throughout this book were taken in the vicinity of the following areas (if more than one on a page read from top to bottom): Contents 5, Haworth (W. Yorks), Ilkley Moor (W. Yorks), Bolton Abbey (Dales), Grassington (Dales); Introduction 6, Hubberholme (Dales); 7, Hawes (Dales); 10, Aysgarth (Dales), Middleham (Dales); 11, Kildale Moor (N. York Moors); 14, Lealholm Moor (N. York Moors); 15, Gillamoor (N. York Moors), Commondale (N. York Moors); 21, Ravenscar (Coast); 23, Dalby (Howardian Hills); 25, Kilnsey (Dales); The National Parks 154, Hutton-le-Hole (N. York Moors); Index 160, Staithes (Coast).

BIBLIOGRAPHY

Addison, Sir William, *The Old Roads of England*, Batsford, London, 1980

Atkinson, J. C., *Forty Years in a Moorland Parish*, Macmillan, London, 1891

Bede, *The Ecclesiastical History of the English Nation*, Dent, London, n.d.

Bogg, Edmund, *From Eden Vale to the Plains of York: A Thousand Miles in the Valleys of the Nidd and Yore*, Bogg, Leeds, n.d.

Booth, R. K., *York: The History and Heritage of a City*, Barrie & Jenkins, London, 1990

Browne, H. B., *Chapters of Whitby History 1823-1946*, Brown, London, 1946

Brumhead, D., *Geology Explained in the Yorkshire Dales and on the Yorkshire Coast*, David & Charles, Newton Abbot, 1979

Bryant, Julius, *Turner Painting the Nation*, English Heritage, London, 1996

Burns, Tom Scott, *Round and About The North Yorkshire Moors (Vol.I)*, M.T.D. Rigg, Leeds, 1987

Burns, Tom Scott, & Rigg, Martin, *Round and About The North Yorkshire Moors (Vol.II)*, M. T. D. Rigg, Leeds, 1988

Camden, William, *Britannia*, Gibson, London, 1695 (1st pub. 1586)

Cobbett, William, *Rural Rides*, Dent, London, 1912

Cockcroft, Barry, (Hannah Hauxwell), *Seasons of My Life*, Century Hutchinson, London, 1989

Defoe, Daniel, *A Tour Thro' the Whole Island of Great Britain*, Davies, London, 1927

Duncombe, C. W. E., *Ryedale*, Ryedale Branch, Council for the Preservation of Rural England, Appleton-Le-Moors, 1951 (1st pub. 1934)

Fawcett, Edward R., *Lead Mining in Swaledale*, Faust, Burnley, 1985

Fletcher, J. S., *The Enchanting North*, Eveleigh Nash, London, 1908

Fletcher, J. S., *A Picturesque History of Yorkshire (3 Vols.)*, Dent, London, 1900

Gaskell, Elizabeth, *The Life of Charlotte Bronte*, O.U.P., Oxford, 1996 (1st pub. 1857)

Gaskell, Elizabeth, *The Life of Charlotte Bronte*, Penguin Books, Harmondsworth, 1975 (1st pub. 1857)

Gee, H. L., *Folk Tales of Yorkshire*, Nelson, London, 1952

Gee, H. L., *The Romance of the Yorkshire Coast*, Methuen, London, 1928

Godfrey, Arthur, & Lassey, Peter J., *Shipwrecks of the Yorkshire Coast*, Dalesman, Clapham, 1989

Graves, John, *The History of Cleveland*, Jollie, Carlisle, 1808

Gunn, Peter, *The Yorkshire Dales*, Century, London, 1984

Hartley, Marie, & Ingilby, Joan, *Getting to Know Yorkshire*, Dent, London, 1964

Hartley, Marie, & Ingilby, Joan, *Life & Traditions in the Moorlands of North-East Yorkshire*, Dent, London, 1972

Hartley, Marie, & Ingilby, Joan, *Life & Traditions in the Yorkshire Dales*, Dalesman, Clapham, 1989

Hartley, Marie, & Ingilby, Joan, *The Yorkshire Dales*, Dent, London, 1956

Hartley, Marie, & Ingilby, Joan, *The Wonders of Yorkshire*, Dent, London, 1959

Hayes, R. H., & Rutter, J. G., *Rosedale Mines & Railway (Research Report No.9)*, Archaeological & Historical Society, Scarborough, 1974

Herriot, James, *James Herriot's Yorkshire*, Michael Joseph, London, 1979

Hiley, Michael, *Frank Sutcliffe Photographer of Whitby*, Gordon Fraser, London, 1974

Hill, David, *In Turner's Footsteps*, Murray, London, 1984

Hill, David, *Turner in the North*, Yale University Press, London, 1996

Hill, David, *Turner in Yorkshire*, York City Art Gallery, York, 1980

House of the North York Moors, H M S.O., London, 1987

Jay, Bill, *Victorian Cameraman: Francis Frith's Views of Rural England 1850-1898*, David & Charles, Newton Abbot, 1973

Jeffrey, Shaw, *Whitby Lore & Legend*, Horne, Whitby, 1923

Kingsley, Charles, *The Water Babies*, Penguin Books, Harmondsworth, 1995 (1st pub. 1863)

Knight, William, (ed.), *Journals of Dorothy Wordsworth*, Macmillan, London, 1930

Lewis, David B., (ed.), *The Yorkshire Coast*, Normandy Press, Beverley, 1991

Linskill, Mary, *Tales of the North Riding*, Macmillan, London, 1898

Macaulay, Lord, *The History of England from the Accession of James II*, Longmans, London, 1880 (1st pub. 1848-61)

Mee, Arthur, *Yorkshire East Riding with York (The King's England series)*, Hodder and Stoughton, London, 1941

Mee, Arthur, *Yorkshire North Riding (The King's England series)*, Hodder and Stoughton, London, 1941

Mee, Arthur, *Yorkshire West Riding (The King's England series)*, Hodder and Stoughton, London, 1941

Mitchell, W. R., & Fox, Peter, *The Story of Ribblehead Viaduct*, Castleberg, Giggleswick, 1990

Morris, John, (ed.), *Domesday Book: Yorkshire (Pts. I & II)*, Phillimore, Chichester, 1986

Ord, John Walker, *The History and Antiquities of Cleveland*, Simpkin & Marshall, Edinburgh, 1846

Pevsner, Nikolaus, *Yorkshire The North Riding (Buildings of England series)* Penguin, Harmondsworth, 1966

Pevsner, Nikolaus, *Yorkshire West Riding (Buildings of England series)*, Penguin, Harmondsworth, 1959

Pevsner, Nikolaus, *Yorkshire: York & The East Riding (Buildings of England series)*, Penguin, Harmondsworth, 1972

Pontefract, Ella, Hartley, Marie, *Yorkshire Tour*, Dent, London, 1939

Raistrick, Arthur, & Illingworth, John L., *The Face of North-West Yorkshire*, Dalesman, Clapham, 1959

Raistrick, Arthur, *Lead Mining in the Yorkshire Dales*, Dalesman, Clapham, 1975

Raistrick, Arthur, *Malham & Malham Moor*, Dalesman, Clapham, 1947

Raistrick, Arthur, (ed.), *North York Moors (National Park Guide No.4)*, H.M.S.O., London, 1969

Raistrick, Arthur, *Old Yorkshire Dales*, David & Charles, Newton Abbot, 1968

Raistrick, Arthur, *The Pennine Dales*, Eyre & Spottiswoode, London, 1968

Raistrick, Arthur, *Vikings, Angles & Danes in Yorkshire*, Dalesman, Clapham, 1965

Ratcliff, Nora, (ed.), *The Journal of John Wesley*, Nelson, London, 1940

Ree, Harry, & Forbes, Caroline, *The Three Peaks of Yorkshire*, Wildwood House, London, 1983

Ruskin, John, *Modern Painters (Vols. I-V)*, Allen, London, 1906 (1st pub.1843-60)

Sedgwick, Adam, *Adam Sedgwick's Dent: A Memorial by the Trustees of Cowgill Chapel (1868) & Supplement to the Memorial (1870)*, Hollett, Sedbergh, 1984

Shanes, Eric, *Turner's England: 1810-38*, Cassell, London, 1990

Shanes, Eric, *Turner's Picturesque Views in England and Wales 1825-1838*, Chatto & Windus, London, 1979

Shaw, Bill Eglon, (comp.), *Frank Meadow Sutcliffe: A, Selection of His Work*, Sutcliffe Gallery, Whitby, 1974

Shaw, Bill Eglon, (comp.), *Frank Meadow Sutcliffe: A Second Selection*, Sutcliffe Gallery, Whitby, 1978

Shaw, Bill Eglon, (comp.), *Frank Meadow Sutcliffe: A Third Selection*, Sutcliffe Gallery, Whitby, 1990

Simmons, I. G., (ed.), *Yorkshire Dales National Park*, H.M.S.O., London, 1971

Smith, Lucy Toulmin, (ed.), *The Itinerary of John Leland*, Southern Illinois University press, Carbondale, 1964

Spratt, D. A., & Harrison, B. J. D., (eds.), *The North York Moors Landscape Heritage*, David & Charles, Newton Abbot, 1989

Staniforth, Alan, *Geology of the North York Moors*, North York Moors National Park, Helmsley, 1990

Steers, J. A., *The Coastline of England & Wales*, Cambridge University Press, Cambridge, 1969

Stoker, Bram, *Dracula*, Wordsworth Editions, Ware, 1993 (1st pub. 1897)

Wainwright, A., *In the Limestone Dales*, Michael Joseph, London, 1991

Wainwright, A., *Pennine Way Companion*, Westmorland Gazette, Kendal, 1968

Wainwright, A., *Walks in Limestone Country*, Westmorland Gazette, Kendal, 1970

Westall, William, *Views of the Caves near Ingleton, Gordale Scar, and Malham Cove in Yorkshire*, Murray, London, 1818

Woodwark, T. H., *The Crosses on the North York Moors*, Whitby Literary & Philosophical Society, Whitby, 1976

Wright, Geoffrey N., *Roads & Trackways of The Yorkshire Dales*, Moorland, Ashbourne, 1985

Wright, Geoffrey N., *The Yorkshire Dales*, David & Charles, Newton Abbot, 1986

Young, Arthur, *A Six Months Tour Through the North of England*, Strachan, Nicoll & Cadell, London, 1771

INDEX

Page numbers in *italics*
refer to illustrations.

Aberford 10
Adam-Salomon, Antony-Samuel 16
Addlebrough 55
All Saints Church, Rotherham 14
All Saint's Church, Rudston 148
Ampleforth Abbey and College 126, 155
Arkengarthdale 67
Askrigg 55

Bainbridge Pastures 55
Baldersdale 71
Batty Moss 51
Beck Hole 130
Bempton Cliffs, near Flamborough 149
Beverley Minster 14
Bishopdale 56
Black Nab, Saltwick Bay 100
Blackstone Edge 8, 10
Blakey Ridge 118, 120
Bolton Abbey 34, 155
Bolton Priory 34
Boroughbridge 8
Boulby Cliff 88
boundary stone, Blakey Ridge 120
Boynton, Sir Griffith 8
Bradford 15
Bransdale 110
Bridestones, Grime Moor 126
Bridgewater, 3rd Duke of 13
Bridgewater Canal 13
Brimham Rocks, Brimham Moor 74
Brindley, James 13
Brontë Parsonage Museum, Haworth 155
'Burnley House', Hutton-le-Hole 124
Burton Agnes 8
Butter Tubs, near Thwaite 57
Butter Tubs Pass 58
Byland Abbey, near Coxwold 155

Calder, River 30
Calder valley 30
canals 13, 18, 25
Captain Cook's Monument 86
Castle Howard, near Malton 6, 141, 155
Castleton Rigg 107
caverns 154
Cawthorn Camps, near Pickering 154
Clapham 46

Cleveland Hills 154
Cleveland Hills Escarpment 83
Cleveland Plain 85, 154
Cleveland Way 154
Clifford's Tower, York 144, 155
Coast to Coast Walk 154
cobles 90
Coke, Thomas William 11
Commondale 19
Commondale Moor 105
Craven, near Settle 17
Creteblock tug 99
crosses 112, 130, 154
Cumbria 6

Daguerre, Louis Jacques Mandé 15
Dalby Forest 154
Danby Dale 108
Danby Head 109, 110, 117
Danby High Moor 113, 114, 117
Davy, Sir Humphry 15
Defoe, Daniel 10
Dentdale, near Cowgill 52
Derbyshire 10
Derwent, River 26
deserted medieval village
    (Wharram Percy) 146, 155
Devil's Arrows, near Boroughbridge 79
Doncaster 8
Druid's Temple, near Ilton 74
drystone walling 154, 156
Duncombe Park, Helmsley 13, 155
Durham 6

Easby Abbey, near Richmond 73, 155
East Mines, Rosedale 120
East Stonesdale, near Keld 68
Edward VII, King 16
Egglestone Abbey, near Barnard Castle
    71, 155
Eller Beck, Beck Hole 130
English Heritage 155
Esk Valley 19

Falling Foss, near Little Beck 132
Farndale 111
Fat Betty, Danby High Moor 113
Fell Beck 154
Fenton, Roger 20
Fiennes, Celia 7, 8, 10
Filey Brigg 149
Flamborough Head 150

Forestry Commission 154
Fountains Abbey 6, 13, 14, 155
Abbot Huby's Tower 76
Nave Aisle 76
Fox Talbot, William Henry 15, 16
Frith, Francis 20
Fylingdales Moor 130

Gaping Gill pothole 154
Gargrave 154
George III, King 11, 13
Gilpin, Reverend William 11
Gisborough Abbey 154
Glaisdale Moor 20
Gordale Scar, near Malham 44, 154
Great Ayton 85
Great Ayton Moor 86
Great Fryup Dale 20
Grime Moor 126
Grinton Moor 56
Gunnerside, Upper Swaledale 63

Hambleton Hills 83, 154
Harewood House, Leeds 6, 11, 14, 34,
    155
Harrogate 8
Hathersage Moor 27
Haworth Parsonage 33
Hebden, River 30
Hebden Bridge 30
Helmsley Castle 21, 154, 155
Hesleden Bergh 38
Higger Tor, Hathersage Moor 27
High Crag 109
High Frith, West Stones Dale 68
highwaymen 7
Hinchliffe Mill 28
Hole of Horcum, Levisham Moor 128
Holmfirth 29
Humber, River 26
Hury Reservoir 71
Hutton-le-Hole 124

Ingleborough *title-page* 48, 154
Ingleby Greenhow 85
Ingleton 23
Ivelet 60, 61

Jervaulx Abbey 73

Keld 67, 68
Kettle Ness 90, 94

Kirkdale 125
Kirkham Priory, Whitwell-on-the-Hill
    146, 155
Kirkstall Abbey, Leeds 14

Lamartine, Alphonse de 15–16
Lancashire 6, 10, 26
Langstrothdale 37, 38
Lascelles, Edward Viscount 11, 14
Lastingham 127
Lealholm Moor 104
Leeds 15
Levisham Moor 128
lighthouse, Flamborough Head 150
Lilla Cross, Fylingdales Moor 130
limestone 17, 23, 154
'Limestone Country', near Settle 17
Lingrow Knock 90
Little Beck Valley 132
Little Blakey Howe 118
Little Fryup Dale 110
Little Hunters Sleets 36
Littondale 38
Loe Moors, Vale of Pickering 139
Low Bridestones, Grime Moor 126
Lower Aysgarth Falls, Wensleydale 57
Lunedale, near Grassholme 70
Lythe 97

McAdam, John Loudon 18
Macaulay, Lord 20
Malham 23, 43
Malham Cove 40, 43, 154
Malham Moor 40
marker stones (Fat Betty, Danby High
    Moor) 113
medieval village, deserted
    (Wharram Percy) 146
Metcalf, John (Blind Jack of
    Knaresborough) 18
Middleham Castle, Wensleydale 73, 155
Middlesbrough 15
'Midge Hall', Little Beck Valley 132
mines 64, 120
Mount Grace Priory, Osmotherley 155

Napoleon Bonaparte 30
National Park Authority 154
National Trust 154, 155
Nevison, William 7
Newton Dale 16
Norber Boulders, near Austwick 47

Norham Castle, Northumberland 11
North Pennine cave area 154
North Sea 152, 154
North York Moors 6, 18
North York Moors National Park 154, 155
North Yorkshire Moors Railway, Newton Dale 16

obelisk (Stoodley Pike) 30
Old Gang Mines, Swaledale 64
Old Ralph Cross, Westerdale Moor 112
Ouse, River 8, 26
Oxnop Side, near Swaledale 63

Peak Steel, Ravenscar 13
Pen-y-ghent 154
Pennine Way 30, 154
Pennines 30, 154
photography 15–16, 19–20, 21, 23, 156
Pickering Castle 138, 154, 155
Plompton Rocks 14
Pontefract 8
Port Mulgrave 90
pot-holes 57, 154
Pry Hill, near Keld 68

Quakers' Trod, near Commondale 104

railways 16, 16, 18, 25
Raven Hall Hotel, Ravenscar 13
Ravenscar 13, 13
Ribblehead Viaduct, Batty Moss 51
Richmond Castle 14, 72, 155
'ridings' 6, 26
Rievaulx Abbey 6, 125, 154, 155
Ripon Cathedral 14
Robin Hood's Bay 13, 135, 137
The Openings 135
rocks 21, 23
Roman road, Bainbridge Pastures 55
Roman road, Blackstone Edge 8
Romans 154
Roseberry Topping 86
Rosedale 120, 122
Rosedale Abbey 154
Rosedale Head 122
Rotherham bridge and chapel 14
Royal Photographic Society 16, 20
Rudston 148
Runswick Bay 93, 94
Ruskin, John 10–11, 14, 19

St Andrew's Church, Ingleby Greenhow 85
St Gregory's Minster, Kirkdale 125
St James Church, Clapham 46
St Mary's Abbey, York 143

St Mary's Church, Thirsk 79
St Mungo's Well, Copgrove, near Ripon 8
St Oswald's Church, Lythe 97
St William's College, York 145
Saltergate Moor 129
Saltwick Bay 100, 103
Sand Hill 19
Sandsend, near Whitby 97
Sandsend Ness 99
Satron Moor 64
Scales Moor, near Ingleton 51
Scarborough 8
Scarborough Castle 137, 155
Semer Water 52
Settrington Beacon 147
sheep 117, 154
Sheffield 15
Sheriff Hutton Castle 140
Shorkley Hill, Malham 44
South Woods, Sutton Bank 80
Souther Scales 48
Spaunton Moor 122
Spindle Thorn 122
'Spout House', Bransdale 110
Staithes 88
Stoodley Pike, near Todmorden 30
The Strid, near Bolton Abbey 35
Studley Royal 155
Temple of Piety 77
Sutcliffe, Frank Meadow 15, 16, 18, 19, 20
Sutcliffe, Thomas 16
Sutton Bank 80, 83
Swaledale 64
Swaledale sheep 117, 154

Tadcaster 8, 10
Talbot, Rob 21, 23
Talbot and Whiteman 21, 23
Tan Hill 154
Tees, River 15, 26
Telford, Thomas 13, 18
Thirsk 79
Thornton Force, near Ingleton 23, 23, 46
Three Peaks Walk 154
Thwaite 60
Top Withens, Haworth Moor 32
Treasurer's House, York 144, 155
trods (Quakers' Trod, near Commondale) 104
Turner, Joseph Mallord William 10–11, 14
turnpike roads 7, 13, 18

Upper Swaledale 58, 60, 63
Upper Wharfedale, near Kettlewell 36

Vale of Mowbray 154
Vale of Pickering 139, 140, 154
Vale of York 18, 154
viaduct (Ribblehead) 51
Victoria, Queen 15, 20

Wadesmill, near Ware, Hertfordshire 7
Wainman's Pinnacle, near Cowling 33
Wainstones 85
Wainwright, Alfred 154
waterfalls 23, 46, 57, 132
Watlowes Dry Valley, Malham Cove 40
Wayworth Moor 105
Wayworth Moor half-title
weaving 30
Wedgwood, Thomas 15
Wensleydale 55, 56, 57, 73
West Stones Dale 68
Westerdale 107
Westerdale Moor 107, 112
Western Howes 107
Wharfe, River 38
Wharfedale 36
Wharram Percy deserted medieval village 146, 155
Wheeldale Moor 154
Whernside 154
Whitby 15, 16, 18, 20
Old Town 100
Whitby Abbey 103, 155
Whitby Harbour 18
Whitby Museum 20
Whitby Scaur 99
White Scars title-page
Wolds, the 140, 147
woods (South Woods, Sutton bank) 80
woollen industry 30
Worsley 13

Yockenthwaite Farm, Langstrothdale 37
York 6, 7, 8, 10, 143
City Walls 143
Clifford's Tower 144
St William's College 145
Treasurer's House 144, 155

York Minster 13, 14, 143
Yorkshire Dales 6, 23, 25
Yorkshire Dales National Park 154, 155
Young, Arthur 13–14
Young Ralph Cross, Westerdale Moor 154